THINKONOMICS

ILLUSTRATED CRITICAL THINKING ARTICLES

ROBERT A JOHNSON

ILLUSTRATED BY CHUCK HARRISON

Ockham
Publishing

Thinkonomics by Robert A Johnson and Chuck Harrison

Copyright © Robert A Johnson and Chuck Harrison 2018

Published by Ockham Publishing in the United Kingdom in 2018

ISBN 978-1-83919-242-5

Cover by Claire Wood

Cover images by Chuck Harrison

www.ockham-publishing.com

CONTENTS

INTRODUCTION	1
SHOULD MUSIC BE FREE?	4
WHAT WILL BECOME OF THE 'GENTLEMAN'S GAME'?	10
WHAT IS 'VISION' AND WHY DO POLITICIANS NOT HAVE IT?	16
IS MASS POLITICAL INVOLVEMENT/PASSION A GOOD THING?	20
WHAT EFFECT DOES 'MEDIA BALANCE' HAVE?	24
ARE NUCLEAR WEAPONS GOOD FOR THE WORLD?	30
CAN A REFUSAL TO USE NUCLEAR WEAPONS RUIN THE DETERRENT?	34
WHY ARE WE ALL SO EASILY FOOLED BY PLACEBOS?	40
SHOULD WE BE PRO-CHOICE OR PRO-LIFE?	44
THE MORAL WORRY IN CRIMINAL ALLEGATIONS THAT WE ALL LIKE TO IGNORE	50
PREJUDICE OR HEALTH PROMOTION?	54
DO WE ASK THE WRONG QUESTIONS ABOUT PUBLIC SERVICES?	58
HOW FAR SHOULD WE EXPAND ETHICS?	62
ARE WE WRONG ABOUT TRANSGENDERISM?	68
WHAT ARE MEN'S RIGHTS ACTIVISTS MISSING?	72
IS SENTIENCE A SPECTRUM?	76
IS SEPARATING RACES THE BEST WAY TO ATTACK RACISM?	82
HOW DO WE ENSURE A NEUTRAL MEDIA?	88
THINGS I BELIEVE THAT ARE PROBABLY FALSE OR CORRELATIONS I HAVE NOT EXAMINED THE CAUSATION FOR	92

DO ANALOGIES WORK?   98

IS CONSCIOUSNESS MYSTERIOUS?   102

CAN COMPUTERS BECOME CONSCIOUS? AND SHOULD WE BE WORRIED?   106

PARADOXES PROBABLY DON'T EXIST   114

DOES THE SUBJECTIVE NATURE OF ETHICS DOOM RATIONAL GOVERNMENT AND ECONOMICS?   120

IS YOUR BRAIN ENTIRELY RELIANT ON CONTEXT?   124

OBSESSION WITH CULTURE OVER HUMANKIND   128

SHOULD THE OLYMPICS BE MODERNISED?   132

WHAT ARE THE RULES OF SATIRE?   140

WHY IS THE ABSURD FUNNY?   146

WHY DO WE EMBRACE LABELS, BUT NOT EVIDENCE?   152

WASTE AND THE BACK OF A SOFA ANALOGY   158

WHAT'S IN A WORD?   164

WHY YOU SHOULDN'T DEMONISE ECONOMIC GROWTH   170

THINKONOMICS

ILLUSTRATED CRITICAL THINKING ARTICLES

INTRODUCTION

There's something innately funny and obvious about human bias. I fail to remember how many comedy sketches I have seen where one person tries in vain to crack a difficult lock, or to cut through a reinforced window, pulling the audience into his immense struggle, whilst his ally looks on – puzzled – right before turning the handle on the unlocked door.

Part of the reason that kind of sketch is so popular is because we relate. We're a species of smart, rational apes, who regularly miscalculate the level or type of reasoning needed for any given situation. We're capable of the most immense achievements imaginable, from space flight to ingenious medical techniques, yet reasonably often we'll set about trying to solve an impossible problem when a simpler way around it was facing us all the time. Likewise, when faced with impossible questions, which should beget uncertainty, we settle for simple, certain answers.

These essays and drawings are a way of celebrating this quirk, but more than that, are an attempt to get you thinking about and questioning all manner of interesting things you may not have realised are even up for debate. From important matters such as politics and economics, or more general topics such as comedy or arts, herein lies a wide variety of critical thinking topics.

But don't be fooled into thinking this is some sort of guide to revolutionary thinking about society; it isn't. Whilst I think some of these short pieces sum up unique and often ignored problems that few actually think about, others are putting a genuine debate across: not because I always disagree with how we currently think about the matter, but because I think we should consider things critically and challenge ourselves to defend our ideas. Even if they were right all along.

There is no necessary connection, from start to finish, other than that each article is putting forward an opinion or a debate which is often ignored or indulged shallowly. I did not plan out this collection thinking "I have something on politics, now I must write a relatable one about TV".

What ties them together is that they all start with a similar situation to that very first comedy sketch I mentioned. As far as I'm concerned, on each of these subjects people are trying desperately to cut through that window – or scale the roof to squeeze down the chimney – when they haven't even considered trying the door. Sometimes, in fact, they're using explosives to blow the windows out, and others didn't even notice the house at all and are setting about a gnome in the garden. All the while, the door was wide open. And occasionally, just occasionally mind you, I'm going to join the other person in banging on the window, because that door was in fact securely locked and chained.

If you take one thing away from this book – whether you agree with all, some or none of the essays in it – let it be that *it never hurts to try the handle.*

SHOULD MUSIC BE FREE?

We seem to be in a regular cycle of debates within the music industry: about whether artists and record labels are paid fairly, about how we should control music piracy, and sometimes about how we should treat those people who 'steal' music online.

Strangely, though unsurprisingly, this entire debate is had on the terms set forth by those who profit most from music itself. Rarely do you hear from artists (of which there are many) who make music which they offer for free, or people who actually listen to and live by music. These groups of people far outnumber those who make it.

Once again, this is not surprising. The well-known artists in the music industry are those who make the most money, as they are the ones who appear on commercials, posters and TV shows, flaunted by the record labels who wish to invest in public advertising as a method of increasing their yield from this year's cash cow. So those with a stronger and more recognisable voice are those most likely to desire the status quo.

We therefore end up in the strange situation of country pop song-stress Taylor Swift and 'perennially famous for the past' Midge Ure discussing the ethics of music sharing, despite not having any experience other than making money from it. A bit like important debates on Euthanasia being held only between ambitious, uncompassionate grandchildren.

Were the debate to be had on the terms of rational ethics, we wouldn't start by asking how best to compensate record companies or artists, but whether they have a naturally assigned right to make money from music at all. That issue is not as straight forward as everyone thinks.

Suppose I manufacture and sell CDs, onto which I have recorded my-self speaking various rhymes to a tune I have played out on my beginner's bass guitar. In keeping with sensible rules in our society, I am wronged if someone steals those CDs. I made them, they belong to me, and I am willing to part with them for whatever amount of cash I deem necessary. To allow someone to steal them would be doing me a disservice.

Suppose, instead, that I wish not to contribute to society in any normal job, but also wish not to produce CDs as I don't have the money to produce them, and instead desire to speak my bass-backed verses into a microphone and then sell the audio file for a living. Are we really saying that, if someone is to share that audio file for free, they have wronged me because it is my voice and my fingers making the bass noises, and I have a right to make a living from it? What gives me this natural sole right to every noise I make – such a desperate necessity, in fact, that people should go to prison for sharing it without me profiting?

This is quite a difficult question. The best way of exploring it is not to single out music, but to place it in context alongside visual media (such as movies and shows) and e-books/comics, and then to explore whether or not it is wrong to share anything which has no physical manifestation of production.

The simple argument – the one that is unanimously agreed within all media industries (including by Swift and Ure, who the media pretends to be both sides of the debate) – is that the internet has changed the game. The relatively obvious rules regarding physical manufacture and stealing governed how we developed and sold music before, but the internet allows people to 'steal' without physically 'stealing'. Thus the same rules of ownership should apply to e-products as apply to physical products, to encapsulate this new form of stealing.

Fine… except… look back at that last paragraph. The argument correctly asserts that the internet has changed the game, but then draws the conclusion from that to be that people can now 'steal' without physically 'stealing'. That's not a logical conclusion, it's an assumption. People can now *share* without physically stealing, but we have to be willing to baselessly assume that this sharing simply *is* stealing, as no material theft is taking place. Sharing does not remove an item which could otherwise be sold, and give it free. Instead it duplicates an audio, visual or text-based file for someone else to enjoy, whilst the original remains untouched.

To assume that this sharing is stealing, is to assume that a set of companies have a natural right to a certain level of profits, regardless of

6

whether or not technology has naturally made the product they produce less profitable. I realise this flies against the company-orientated logic of modern society, so perhaps an example would help to make my point.

It is not illegal to go home and sew the pips of an apple in your garden to produce more apples. Mr Del Monte will not be sending you cease and desist letters if you grow a banana in a similar way (though, some select forms of GM crop reproduction do result in such legal threats but that is another matter). And, were we able to use new technology to sew Sainsbury's apple seeds into a daily apple dispenser, which amazingly grew apples daily for us to eat for free, Sainsbury's would have no ethical or legal right to chase us for 'stealing' from their fruit industry. So there is little logical precedent to consider the similar situation – the duplication of e-files – to be a horrendous moral act.

An alternative and more technologically capable model of media, in fact, exists: digital media being widely, freely available, whilst people can still buy physical or legitimate/convenient copies (such as through iTunes), and artists can make money from gigs, concerts, shows, merchandising, screenings etc. Many artists already embrace and work within this model: check out *bandcamp* or similar sites for huge swathes of bands that do. Do we really believe that artists are precious flowers who can only create good music if they are picked up by a record label, or surrounded by an entourage – funded by the selling of e-files – or do we believe that some people have talent, and those people can make a name for themselves and succeed based on that talent in a fair market place? If you're a music fan, you surely agree with the latter, else you have a very pessimistic view of that which you support.

This alternative system is different in one major respect: it leaves little room for record labels to have power or to profit to the levels they currently do. In a world where media is freely digitally available, the surplus millions for these companies drop off, and music is primarily decided upon by the listener or the advocate, rather than the advertising campaigns. Artists are rewarded more fairly and without huge cuts going to companies that control the flow of cash into music.

What's more, how many of us would want to download Taylor Swift, if it wasn't for the ad campaigns, glossy magazine covers and hyped up videos? The millions deemed appropriate to spend on these things would suggest that not many of us would if we weren't persuaded by the daily marketing. So we may well end up being lured into listening, then morally reprimanded for doing so without paying, despite no theft taking place. There's a serious problem with this reasoning.

It's no wonder record companies are the one's fighting tooth and nail to keep the old methods, despite the rise of 'piracy'. A rise, even whilst it is currently discouraged through law. But we should never have been listening to the debate on their terms in the first place: we are all stake-holders with an interest in the diverse and important world of music, and how sounds and noises are governed. Companies that make music should produce it on fair terms or not at all. If that means Taylor Swift has to work in an office during the day at the start of her career, before she makes a name based on talent, so be it.

As horrified as I am that these precious musicians might have to live around the rest of us – shocking, I know – my ethical reasoning can make peace with it.

WHAT WILL BECOME OF THE 'GENTLEMAN'S GAME'?

There are two problems that immediately spring to mind when you see a title like that. Firstly, writing in 2015, what on earth is so special about any game that makes it so gender specific? Surely it isn't a game related directly to, and accessible only by, genitalia.

Secondly, most people know the "gentleman's game" is a traditional term that refers to cricket, which is a sport. And those of us that watch or play any sport, occasionally have that awakening of self-realisation, where we suddenly become conscious that we are doing nothing more than trivial and bizarre tasks, performed in an ultra-competitive manner.

Hitting a round lump of cork with a large piece of tree, not allowing it to go behind you and hit the further three wooden sticks that you are desperately striving to protect, is not a sensible thing for any adult to be doing. But then, alas, neither is shoving parts of your body into/on top of someone else's in an affectionate manner, in order that you might create little genetic replications of yourselves that you will spend the next 18 years trying to mould into something like you. Sport, thus, is hardly more bizarre than even the most lauded of human activities.

My intention in this piece is not so much to point out that games are odd in general or that cricket necessarily is either, but to point to one of its bizarre quirks.

Like many sports, the last few decades have seen cricket increasingly populated by super fit athletes; personalities described best by terms like 'driven' or 'by any means necessary'. Yet it has still maintained a sense of decency, a gentleman-like environment. Cricketers can be banned for swearing or even just disagreeing with an umpire, whilst there are regular pundit-led discussions about 'the spirit of the game' like we see in no other sport.

In the past, this 'spirit of the game' has been pretty loosely defined, but can essentially be defined as an attitude of honesty among the players. For instance, on decisions regarding *catches*. For those uninitiated types, a catch is a method of a batsman getting 'out' (meaning they are done for this part of the game, and must return to the dressing room, leaving the batting to other team members who have yet to get 'out' –

everyone on your team gets a go at batting, until there's only one batsman left). To be 'caught out' the ball must hit your bat or your hand, and then be caught by an opposition team member before it touches the ground.

Sometimes an umpire can't be sure if a fielder, who could be 50 metres away, caught the ball before it touched the ground (so isn't a 'catch'). Similarly, they may not know if the batsman just hit the ball with a tiny edge of the bat, or didn't hit it at all. In the past, the 'spirit of the game' taught youngsters to just 'walk' if you have hit the ball and been caught out, not even waiting for the umpire to rule you as out. It also taught fielders to tell the umpire if they did not catch the ball cleanly before it touched the ground.

This kind of honesty has understandably been challenged by the ultra-competitive, lucrative, sponsorship-fuelled world of modern cricket. Batsmen who clearly hit the ball into a fielder's hands have been known to turn to look at the umpire to check that they noticed, whilst fielders can be shown to be wrongly appealing for a catch despite the ball rolling along the ground before they touched it. Of course, one can't be sure that any player is being dishonest, but it seems likely.

It is difficult to back up the claims that the 'spirit of cricket' now shines dimmer than it used to, though it is certainly an appealing argument. Similarly, it seems inevitable. When cricket was played by aristocrats who didn't need the money, or by working class folks for fun, there wasn't a desperate desire to cheat or be dishonest.

I'm sure it must have happened even then occasionally, but the honour and honesty of teaching children the 'spirit' seems reasonably well matched with its opposition of competitive instinct. A fair battle between your raised desire to be honest and honourable, and your natural desire to compete and win. But when the lucrative salaries and sponsorship of modern sport are involved, the battle suddenly seems skewed in favour of winning rather than playing fairly. Competitive instinct becomes a hulking great monster, overcoming that desire to be fair.

Furthermore, as well as being inevitable, this change may be unimportant. Cricket is just a game of using pieces of wood to arbitrarily protect other pieces of wood. It doesn't matter. We might get passionate about it, but the intentions involved in defending the piece of wood, or catching the sphere made of cork, is largely irrelevant. It is still just a game, whatever the rules.

Isn't the important factor about fairness, though? We might reflect on the changing nature of sport – exemplified so obviously by the continuing transformation of cricket – as being detrimental to society. Do we want to be interacting with honest people, or with people who explicitly think about using us in whatever way will best achieve the outcome they want? More to the point, does sport even have this effect, or do people see it as a collection of games that are just fun? Is sport completely removed from how we act in society?

The answer, I would wager, is somewhere in the middle. Of course it's just a game, and of course cheating sportsmen aren't a sign that we are all becoming cheating, dishonest people. But the worry is that the effect that sponsorship and money is having in cricket, in particular, Is all too symptomatic of the risks it poses to society. The defenders of the current structures will say that this money is necessary, either to 'keep up' with other countries or else to create successful teams. But the entire point of sport, or so we like to teach our kids, is that it's the taking part that counts.

We like to think that learning sport is about learning honour, or teamwork, perhaps even strategy and thus critical thinking; about trying your hardest and testing yourself, whilst learning dedication. When sport evolves to be an 'anything goes' pursuit, some of that virtue will remain; the best will still often be those with new and better techniques, or dedication to put the time in. But we do risk losing the respectful, perhaps most honourable parts. The process of learning and playing is partly a goal in itself, and once we lose that in favour of the singular goal of winning, we seem to lose a lot of value.

We need to ask ourselves whether we would rather see our national teams competing at the highest level, or sacrifice a little bit of success for a longer goal: perhaps seeing our batsmen walk before they are ordered 'out', which might cost us the odd win, but will teach the new generation that winning isn't everything. The relatively short-lived pride of victory, playing a conceptually arbitrary game, seems less important than the life lessons that children or adults can learn from the goal of playing sport in itself.

The example of English cricket, in fact, goes even further down this dividing line of success vs wider effect. English cricket experienced its most popular levels for decades in 2005, when they won a popular series vs Australia (called the Ashes) on national free-to-air TV. The media and large audiences were hooked throughout, and the players subsequently each received national honours. Around this height of interest, the ECB (English Cricket Board) had signed a lucrative new contract with pay-to-watch satellite television, meaning following series were watched by far less people, whilst attention to the sport waned.

Free-to-air channels could not compete with the fee that satellite TV could muster, and the ECB said such a deal was necessary; the sport was now popular enough to get them this hugely increased satellite TV money, and as a result more money could be pumped into grass roots cricket. But, of course, as the years went on, fewer youngsters were wanting to play cricket, as it was no longer something they were exposed to on accessible television.

Many pundits, to this day, wonder if this was one of the great mistakes of English cricket; whilst the team have had some success, many theorise this success was sown in and before 2005, and that the lack of youngsters involved in the game will actually reduce the success of the national team in the long-term. The argument is persuasive, for obvious reasons. After all, your academy could be expensive and top of the range, but if the next potential legendary batsman never thinks about playing the sport – having never become attached to it – then you won't be able to train him. The ECB will argue their 'outreach' is now better than ever, and that they now involve themselves in more school programs, but the point remains: will youngsters be attracted to cricket by the occasional coaches appearing at school, or to football or pop music on TV?

Sport, it would seem, has a lot of lessons to learn. Is short-term success always, or even often, allied to long-term success? What is the point of sporting success in the first place, if it's creating a wider society which is less appealing to us? Perhaps the people running these sports nationally should be more culturally accountable; focusing on wider social goals, rather than overarchingly pursuing 'the win', which, however you look at it, seems like a ridiculous goal for any popular cultural phenomena in modern society. We know these things affect our kids, and we should be aware that arbitrary sporting victories aren't as important as the type of world our children will be adults in.

EDIT: since writing this piece, the ECB has agreed a deal to allow terrestrial TV (the BBC) to show ten domestic "Twenty20" matches and two international "Twenty20" matches from the year 2020 (don't get confused). This is arguably an implicit agreement that mistakes have been made, and a step in the right direction, but the likes of world class cricket events, such as the World Cup or England vs Australia 'Ashes' series are not planned to be shown on free-to-air TV.

WHAT IS 'VISION' AND WHY DO POLITICIANS NOT HAVE IT?

21ST CENTURY VISION.

Martin Luther King Jr had it, so did Gandhi, whilst we all seem to think that our current politicians lack it. But what is vision?

When you consider what it really means to have vision (the inspirational kind, not eyesight) you'll likely get different answers from different people. Some might see it as an ability to foresee how certain actions now will affect future outcomes, where others might see vision as the ability to see a time when a new truth becomes widely accepted.

The former definition is something akin to mysticism, if you're spiritually inclined, or economics if you're not. The latter is actually just a confidence in one's own beliefs/reasoning: that one has discovered a 'truth' which will become accepted once others see it. Within society, we split this latter type of visionary further into two groups: arrogant and stubborn, or courageous and driven (which are often only divided by perception, given that people who are 'driven' must also be pretty stubborn, and courage often involves arrogance in one's own beliefs). Still, the magnificence of the term 'vision' means these boring definitions aren't always enough.

If we were to point out people from history that we deem to have vision, we would almost unanimously be using the second definition. People like King and Gandhi championed causes which had not yet been widely accepted but were rationally justified, rather than foreseeing any amazing catalyst, or making complex predictions. Vision, in this sense, is about courage and certainty as much as accepting a future vision.

Yet, the way we use the term nowadays seems like we're asking for something different. Whether in the leaders' debates or media coverage during elections, we seem to decry our politicians for lacking vision. Yet this is arguably the one thing they do not lack, in the UK at least. Between Labour and the Conservatives, we have two very different visions of how society should look: encompassing social welfare and workers' rights vs minimal government intervention and increasing rights for those pursuing profit, respectively (for the good of all, of course). These are visions. Since electing a Conservative government here in the UK in 2015, they have fought tooth and nail to start to dismantle the National Health

Service, and reduce the funding to the BBC. Like it or not, these are people working towards a vision.

The politicians seem as confused about the criticism of lacking vision as anyone else. The Conservatives, as a result, strive to appeal to both visions: a vision of social justice as well as corporate security. Whilst Labour does likewise, reinventing themselves annually as the champion of budget cuts as well as the people. If anything, modern politics has a vision surplus.

Perhaps this is the problem. Perhaps we don't truly believe that you can have both. So by appealing to be everything to everyone, the parties begin to lack a clear vision of what society is meant to be. Those that actually look for vision then turn to the parties on either side who actually don't provide the compromise (hence the rise of the multiparty system in the UK). This means a rise in right and left extremism.

I think the problem goes deeper than this, though. If we look back at figures from history who we believe cut a figure of great vision, we see people who provided uncomfortable truths. Politicians and social leaders who taught the public and fought for what was right, rather than being led in circles by what the public or the media want to hear on a daily basis. Politicians used to be elected on their vision, whereas now we prefer that they just do what we currently want… whilst complaining that they have no vision.

The modern world is strikingly devoid of characters who we can point to as having vision, though that's only because they are scared to tell us what their true vision is. We made that happen. We no longer allow politicians the role of the visionary, instead ensuring they are our servants: to represent public opinion exactly as it is, so that it may never be led from the exact set of beliefs we have right now.

There's no reason, however, to be pessimistic. This is the way things are, not the way they must always be. The Labour Party, at the moment, has a chance of reinventing itself as a party of vision. They will not please everyone by championing the systems of welfare and health care, once more, and providing a stern tax rise for the rich. They may not even be able to regain power immediately in five years. But they will have put in place a strong foundation – a constant, core support – and more importantly, a vision with which to permanently win hearts and minds going forwards. People will grow tired of cruelty, but they've already grown tired of the slightly less cruel 'everything to everyone' option as a vision of betterness. This is the chance not just for a different approach in the next election, but for permanent social change for the better.

IS MASS POLITICAL INVOLVEMENT/PASSION A GOOD THING?

It's difficult, near impossible, for a subject to receive critical analysis, if that critical analysis stands squarely against an obvious public agreement. Yet, here goes. Is it actually a good thing for people to be involved in politics en masse?

We know why it is considered to be a positive thing. Put simply, people having a regular say/interest in how they are governed is good: it is supposed to mean that they aren't duped as easily, or that they care more about important things – like welfare or economics – rather than making voting decisions based on only their individual interests.

This all seems to be a little assumptive, though. Perhaps even outdated. We live in a world where the tabloid media, as the UK's 2015 general election showed, still have a massive influence on what the voters think. And given that political involvement/passion in the modern world means little more than political party advocacy and activism, is it a good thing when people get involved with politics?

In case you were wondering, that's not my whole argument. Though I think it is an interesting reason to doubt our perceived wisdom; I think, generally, a population which is apathetic to politics is going to be of a worse political balance than one that is passionate about it.

The rise of left and right extremism led by the media – which is perhaps partly related to the perceived lack of vision among moderate political parties (as mentioned in the previous essay) – is one reason to doubt whether political engagement is necessarily a good thing. However, a better argument can be encapsulated in one word: economics.

As I write this, the UK is preparing itself for a referendum on whether to leave the EU, which is largely an economic decision. The effects of such a separation are not as big as if a country which had adopted the Euro was holding a referendum, however they are still huge and primarily financial. They relate to how trade would change in various ways (trade agreements, import/export costs, loss of easy international markets, etc) but also areas like immigration, which are primarily focused around whether our welfare bill would be cut, our unemployment rate would change, etc.

These are all factors that someone working in an office, a factory, or even a sports field or entertainment arena, are not well placed to judge. We can know about which areas would be affected in the result of an EU exit, but most people do not thoroughly understand how interest rates affect economic growth, let alone grasp the effects of EU market changes or trade agreements.

Economists can't perfectly predict the future either, of course, but they are in a much better position to judge whether or not an EU exit is beneficial. Asking the public to judge the important and wide-ranging effects of minute details of trade and economics is bizarre, to say the least.

And whilst economics might demonstrate the point well, it isn't just about economics. We aren't well informed, in fact, on most issues. At election time, the media/political/public opinion circle focuses on immigration in a way that is massively disproportionate to its rational affect. Whilst the wealthy and large corporations get away with tens, potentially hundreds, of billions in tax cuts, tax havens and corporate theft and bailouts, the focus on them is minimised and perceived as unimportant, whilst everyone is up in arms about a Lithuanian guy getting a job on a building site ahead of the locally born applicant.

I certainly don't wish to say that the issue of immigration isn't important for the individual who doesn't get the job on the building site. It is, and it should be. And there are areas where immigration is a genuine problem. But the problem is of limited importance, whereas the spending of funds on wealthy individuals to help them avoid paying a proportional higher share in taxes etc, are issues we should all be discussing more frequently, as the effect is greater.

Similarly, this is also not to say that we should rise corporate and wealth tax so high that we remove incentives and collapse the economy altogether. People would then lose jobs, poverty would rise, and we create problems for ourselves unintentionally. The path to hell is paved with good intentions. But this awkward balance about corporate taxation, coupled with the popular yet relatively unimportant topic of immigration, shows exactly the point I am trying to make: normal voters are not well positioned to make these kinds of decisions. Even if we had the balance right, it would be by accident, as we simply don't have the facts and understanding to make the decision.

There are potential solutions to the problem of a perennially under informed electorate (the next essay on media balance delves into this) however it does beg us to consider whether or not we actually want increased political involvement, when the public may be swaying politicians further from rationality than they would otherwise be. Perhaps voting, grudgingly, for a perceived 'boring' political party every five years is actually better for society than mass political engagement in between. Perhaps there's no difference either way, and our media led bias is simply replacing the natural bias of less scrutinised politicians. Which leaves us in a corridor of intellectually stale decisions, if ever I've seen one. Progress is most likely in an altogether new system.

WHAT EFFECT DOES 'MEDIA BALANCE' HAVE?

In another essay in this book, I wrote about the problem with a media that is not independent and neutral. I think it's a huge problem, as in large, democratic societies we rely on the media to be unbiased and truthful. If it becomes controlled by any individual or set of individuals, or if it sways from independence and truth, we essentially begin making poor decisions when electing governments or making other big decisions. We need to accurately know what we are voting for, what's true, and what's complete nonsense or impossibility.

However, mainstream British TV – which is a big part of our media – is a lot better than almost anywhere else in the world. The taxpayer funded BBC and trust-owned Channel 4, as well as the commercially owned ITV, all do a reasonably good job of not taking sides. They don't tend to support particular political parties, or at least they don't explicitly do so. It is a world away from American media giants like Fox, whose right-wing bias and general ignorance of facts is well known around the world.

The problem, though, is the British media have a very poor definition of balance. And there are two brilliant modern examples that show why.

In 2014, one of the countries here in the UK – Scotland – held a referendum on whether it should be independent from the rest of the UK or not. The case for becoming independent was tenuous to say the least, at least from an economic or political standpoint, but some people were passionate in support of a 'yes' vote from the start. Depending on the poll you look at, the support for independence up to the date of the referendum's announcement seemed to be somewhere around 25-30% of the electorate.

Then something strange but, looking back, quite predictable happened. The major TV news coverage was exactly even between the two sides, which is what broadcasters believe to be 'balance', and the polls gradually shifted toward the 'yes' vote until the final days before the election when some polls seemed to suggest a 'yes' vote actually had a slender two or three point lead. Then, funnily enough, it seemed to swing back just enough to balance again. The vote on the night of the referendum finished 45-55 in favour of 'no'. But that's some swing, given the issue of independence had been on the table for decades, and yet the swing from 25% to 45% had only taken a year.

On its own, that's not remarkable. You might expect for there to be a swing towards a good set of arguments when those arguments are on TV every day (even though the good arguments were few and far between from either side…). However, consider this second entirely separate issue, which was the subject of the UK's very next referendum. In 2015, the prime minister announced he would be holding a UK-wide referendum on EU membership – to decide whether we should remain or leave. The exact same thing happened as in Scotland's case.

Again, 'leave' voters rarely got past 30/35% until the magic date of the announcement came. Indeed, when polled as to what they would vote if the UK government said it was happy with the terms of its renegotiation with the EU (which it did), only around 25% said they would vote leave. Funnily enough, the same pattern emerged. That 25% swelled right up to 50% in the last few weeks, and in the very last few days pushed back down to a slim 'remain' vote. The result on the morning of 24th June, as the referendum finished, was a narrow victory for 'leave' which again had pulled 20-30% from nowhere just on the back of the few months of the campaign.

Again, this might be a coincidence. It's difficult to say for certain if this is meaningful evidence at all, but in my opinion it is, as it seems to correspond with the problem we have in the UK. We have tabloids and broadsheets that are corporately owned and always veer right. We have an independent section of usually centre-left leaning but rather talented broadsheets that champion not veering much at all. And the most listened to sections of the media – the broadcasters – stay ruthlessly neutral to the degree that they will only call out lies on one side of the debate if they can find a lie to call out on the other.

This latter point seems to be making the difference in referendums, as it seems to veer public opinion to the right – from the left or centre – but also toward an even split. The independence referendum was entirely characterised by perspectives rather than facts, as 'fear against hope', when in reality it was the known and imperfect versus the unknown and obviously risky. But broadcasters don't have an opinion. They don't see balance as only telling the truths on each side, they simply spread an equal amount of propaganda from each side. In the debates, for instance, the EU referendum saw ITV and BBC employ 'fact checkers' to come and weigh in at the end. But they didn't point out all the major lies, or say which side was making more stuff up, they simply shared out an equal and small number of debunked ideas from each side. And even those were done almost apologetically.

As a result, rather than fair elections, and fair votes, we have ruthlessly equal elections, and votes in which no one is either motivated to tell the truth, or called out for manipulating it. Even votes where a clear majority is known months beforehand, can be ruthlessly swung toward an even split, where the status quo will usually edge it at the last minute (as is human instinct). This doesn't seem like a good way to be doing politics, but it's media that is the problem.

I don't just need to trot out the referendum polls as evidence either. The last two general elections have also shown this – leads that slowly evaporate between the two big parties, with one (2010) ending as an entirely hung parliament (no majority) and needing a coalition government, whilst the other – where polls held an influence themselves by telling voters it would be Labour as king makers in another hung parliament – giving us a status quo led, tiny Tory majority.

How do we do things differently? Well we need independently owned media. But broadcasters and media alike also have to do things differently. One of the most wonderful TV shows of the past decade was HBO's *The Newsroom*, in which a team of skilled and knowledgeable political journalists decided to do media a different way. They held debates, they interviewed figures, and they championed balance. But, yet, they didn't dole out equal amounts of debunking when one party was at it more than the others, and they weren't afraid to say when one party was being particularly dishonest.

This would be real, ruthless neutrality: moderators who step in during debates and make the audience aware that the last point simply isn't true, by using facts and figures, as well as simple rational analysis; teams of fact checkers in their ears who are well-educated, well-read and smart enough to spot absolute drivel that a politician is feeding to the masses; ex-debaters and ex-political candidates, perhaps, with no agenda other than the reward of journalistic integrity.

It's not easy, of course. Even in *The Newsroom*, this depended on Jeff Daniels' character, who was a law graduate with oodles of high court experience, able to interrogate those he interviewed. But these people do exist. We shouldn't care how good or authoritative they seem, we should care about how well they know their stuff, and how big a hole they can rip into a bad argument. This is pretty much the only way to hold politicians to account: a neutral media, and politicians who have to take part in reasoned debates, with expert moderators. The best of those moderators being utilised by the most popular media outlets.

Politicians don't want this, though. They currently think they can wheel some smarmy and/or charming guy in a nice suit, or someone who used to be in the army, or occasionally someone who is known for being a womaniser but somehow has charisma, and you will vote for them. They think this because it's true: they don't need to stand up to reasoned and really balanced debate, and they don't have to have arguments which can withstand complex, rational scrutiny, as the media doesn't have any. They simply have to find attractive ways of answering certain questions, and ways of excusing their lack of answers to others. In a complex world like this – where we don't each understand the ins and outs of economics – that is enough to win them elections. We need expert moderators, and rational balance in media outlets to change to a better way of doing things.

And one day some bright spark – whether it's Robert Peston on ITV or whoever – will amass a team of expert moderators like this, and change society in a way we all want and need it to be changed. Until then we should campaign for and pester him about it (sorry, Robert).

ARE NUCLEAR WEAPONS GOOD FOR THE WORLD?

Every so often, I take a step back and wonder what my younger self would make of what I am writing today. Were he to read the title above, followed by the paragraphs below, he would no doubt be a little shocked. Yet I hope he would learn something new.

To him, it would seem relatively obvious that nuclear weapons aren't a good thing. Of everything humankind has produced, nuclear weapons have a potential for destruction that make our centuries of religious wars look almost insignificant. Just one nuclear bomb could wipe out an entire capital city. A handful could completely obliterate a medium sized country in just a few hours, depending on where they are being launched from. Similarly, the environmental fallout of multiple nuclear bombs could feasibly wipe out most intelligent life from Earth.

I wouldn't argue with this. A very basic analysis says that the existence of nuclear weapons is a risky one.

However, it was in the mid-1940s, during the end of World War 2 – the last great global war – where they were last, and only ever, used. Since then we have seen multiple conflicts around the world, both civil and international, as well as various 'invasions' by countries like the US and Russia who both have nuclear weapons. Yet no one has used them.

Perhaps more surprising is that in the 70 years since the end of World War 2, the US and the USSR have engaged in a 'cold war' where tensions seemed to increase to boiling point, yet still no nuclear weapons were used. Despite the fact that during the Cuban missile crisis it seemed almost certain they would be. The threat was always there, but no war between these two huge nations ensued at all. Indeed conflict here was avoided altogether, perhaps due to the nuclear deterrent.

Many economists think there is a good reason for this. Human history is generously sprinkled with situations where great nations fought each other over territory, resources, or sometimes just pride. These, in fact, are the bloodiest conflicts of all, as they often drag in allies, occupied territories, and other countries stuck in the middle. The Second World War, which is a terrifying example of this, came quickly after the First

World War, which led to a great fear of a third when US and Soviet relations became tense during the cold war period.

No world war grew out of the cold war, and indeed none have appeared since. Wars have happened, but normally focused on one smaller country, with the frequency of combat greatly reduced compared to the early 20th and previous centuries. And many think this is precisely because of nuclear weapons.

Russia, for instance, would not attack the US – regardless of what else happens – as it knows a war with a fellow nuclear power would no longer just be a gradual incline of troops and combat. The US, similarly, thinks the same. War between these nations today would mean a rapidly escalating, catastrophic nuclear assault, one which suits neither presidents' ego nor desperation to be remembered, let alone risky pragmatic consequences. So in this sense, it can be argued that nuclear weapons keep the peace in a way that wasn't possible before.

But the effect doesn't stop there. Countries like the UK also have a nuclear deterrent now, and as much as we all wince at that word – deterrent – it makes sense. The US has many more than the UK, but that it has even one is enough to make it a worthwhile ally under almost any circumstances. Thus Russia would never attack the UK. Indeed many nations now fit into this category – attached ally, or holding a deterrent – to the degree that a world war ever happening again is doubtful.

Does this mean that Russia will immediately leave the Ukraine alone? Or that the US will not embark on more regular, though questionable, Middle East offences? No, probably not. But these kinds of wars always happened; they are something to be solved and done away with.

Nuclear weapons have greatly reduced the much larger loss of life through helping to avoid world wars. Of course they pose important moral questions: what if a more religiously influenced country got a hold of one, for instance, and thus could use it for spiritual or jihad purposes, without thinking as the rational human mind does (as game theory suggests)? That's always going to be a concern. In these circumstances the 'game theory', which stops the US or Russia from ever using their warheads, goes out of the window: consequences and rationality would be sacrificed for religious dogma and a belief in positive post-life-consequences. But right now we must also consider the millions of lives we have likely saved simply by different countries 'owning', but never using, the nuclear deterrent.

In this sense, it has truly been a deterrent, and we would require a well thought through alternative if we were to do away with them. If nuclear weapons aren't ever used, but do act as a deterrent to massive wars, then that's a strong argument in their favour. But does it overcome the risk that a non-democratic and naive else fundamentally religiously-guided country could get hold of one?

So long as lives matter, arguably they matter more than the increasingly abstract risk that nuclear weapons appear to pose.

In the 2015 and 2017 general elections, we saw the left and right political persuasions in the UK discussing the 'waste' of money that nuclear weapons provide, how it could be spent better, and how it could never be used anyway and thus is not a deterrent. I think if you understand why the risk of immediately massive and obliterating negative consequences matters, infinitely more than the risk of gradually increasing amounts of conflict, then you understand why nuclear weapons play a role in keeping peace. It then becomes a difficult, utilitarian calculation if we decide to put a cost on that amount of life.

Sorry, younger me, there is a debate to be had on nuclear weapons – about the ethics of saving lives which we could not otherwise save – which flies in the face of leftist dogma. Nuclear weapons are a risk but, arguably, it is a *guarantee* that many more lives will be lost without them. There has seldom been a debate more difficult and complicated.

CAN A REFUSAL TO USE NUCLEAR WEAPONS RUIN THE DETERRENT?

In the previous article, I put across the argument that nuclear weapons may be a great force for peace, and while I don't think that argument is watertight, it is one of the great debates of our time. It is persuasive that world wars have not occurred since major players obtained nuclear weapons, and the threat they pose means that the occurrence of war has lessened since then.

Whether or not you agree with that statement (this, of course, is the point of the book: to help you think about solutions, not necessarily give you them) you almost certainly see that this is a strong argument which, in 100 years' time, might have borne some significant, lasting evidence in its favour.

However, what if the person in charge of using the nuclear weapon were to publicly state they would never use it? Wouldn't that completely defeat the object of having it as a deterrent?

This was the focus of an enormous amount of public attention in the UK in late 2015, which resurfaced in the hastily arranged general election of 2017, as Jeremy Corbyn, the leader of the opposition in the UK parliament (and a long-time supporter of nuclear disarmament), publically declared he would never 'push the button' if he were in charge.

Cue hysteria among the political right and the senior armed forces. Expert Generals and cabinet ministers alike piped up on news channels 24/7 to say that this would endanger Britain by defeating the object of having a deterrent. It would no longer be a deterrent, they claimed, and a Corbyn-led Labour party would greatly threaten national security. The final 2017 leaders' debate – in which Corbyn took answers from a Question Time audience – allowed various members of the public the chance to publicly reprimand Corbyn for his unwillingness to launch an a-bomb on 'them' who might do it to us. As Corbyn gained ground in the polls, eventually forcing a hung parliament, this negative metaphorical castration by the right-leaning members of the audience may just have stopped Corbyn becoming prime minister.

What we didn't hear, at any point, was anyone actually challenging this assumption. Those defending Corbyn did so by notifying us of the risks of nuclear war – the widespread devastation it would cause – and occasionally by pointing out he was either 'just being honest' or 'just being rational' (I'm paraphrasing the sentiments of Corbyn's allies and CND members alike). On the infamous Question Time debate, this defence came in the form of a young woman aghast at the debate itself, asking: 'I don't know why everyone is so obsessed with killing millions of people?'

So, is it possible to defend the idea that one can refuse to use nuclear weapons whilst maintaining them as a deterrent? Like almost everything else in this book, the answer is a resounding and surprising 'probably'.

To think about this issue more clearly, think about why nuclear deterrents are effective – if they are effective – in the first place. Person A has a weapon as huge, automatic and potentially disastrous as Person B; either side will know if the other uses theirs, and will have time to use their own in response. As far as the idea of deterrence goes, this is just about perfect; even if your opponent has more than you, the damage that even one nuclear warhead could cause – wiping out hundreds of thousands of people in one drop – creates a deterrence which we have never seen any leader ignore.

Does it make a difference whether Person A has two or ten nuclear deterrents? Arguably, no. Other than it being a signifier of other matters – i.e., a country with ten is likely to be larger and have more people – we have yet to see any evidence that any number of warheads is more effective, other than as a matter of status. The reason for that seems pretty simple; if you're willing to risk 400,000 lives immediately with one aggressive decision, you are likely to risk 600,000 or 800,000 too.

Game theorists might be able to specify certain levels of deterrence, in which countries are acting aggressively as a matter of defence, where they can define minor differences in deterrence level per numbers of warheads. However, this is nowhere near to the difference between zero and one nuclear weapon, or, at best, between one and two. Why are two important? Well it's not as important as stepping to one rather than zero. But if you have two nukes, you could use one and still have one left. If the world really has gone to shit, having two means you still have a deterrent even after having encountered the unthinkable.

It seems odd, though, to start needing insurance, on an insurance, on an insurance, when the entire point of the insurance was to be deterrent. The odds have gotten pretty long by this point on how effective the third deterrent really is; if you've already used two nuclear weapons, odds are you've already deterred as much as you can deter. If you need a third, it's not clear how much difference you're creating, as you're encountering an opponent who no amount of deterrence will seemingly account for; you might as well be fighting suicide bomber aliens of unknown intention. Your population is arguably no better defended by having three than two.

So there is good reason to believe that the number of warheads above one, or perhaps two, is reasonably irrelevant (if you remove geographical limits, that is; obviously you can't always have two that are positioned to hit any other country in the world, in which case you might need many, or else a constantly, mysteriously moving one, like the UK does). This tells us that in terms of the game theory, it is merely having a deterrent that is the deterrent: having more of it makes little difference, so long as your opponent believes it can hit them.

Is game theory changed, though, if one of the players maintains they would never use the deterrent? Arguably, no, as by virtue of countries considering them a deterrent, they already implicitly make the same claim. By calling nuclear warheads a deterrent and not a constructive weapon, and by only one in the history of the world ever being used, they already imply 'we don't want to use this unless you make us use it, by using your own'. Evidence of this appears every time Russia or the USA invades land with troops or airstrikes but without a hint of nuclear weaponry.

By saying 'I would never use it', you are saying you could not foresee a situation where you would use it yourself. That's no different to anyone else, if everyone else is already implying 'I would use it, but only if you do'. Unless someone explicitly says: 'I would happily nuke someone just to be aggressive', then saying 'I would never use it, unless you do' isn't actually different to 'I would never use it'.

Am I being too simplistic by pointing to the logic? Am I ignoring the real world effect? Well let's consider it. Imagine you are Obama or Putin and you have nuclear warheads. In fact, imagine you are any world leader, with any amount of nuclear warheads. Imagine you know Britain has two warheads. Now imagine a man is elected in Britain who has verbally *said* he refuses to ever use his warheads. He still has two, but refuses to use them. Do you suddenly feel a bit safer from him? Perhaps. But do you now cross Britain off the list of potential nuclear opponents? Of course not.

Human beings, especially politicians, reverse decisions all the time. Governments change all the time. And both lie, constantly. Decisions can reverse in a matter of hours; coups can happen in minutes; Corbyn can change his mind in seconds; he could have been lying all along; he could have been playing a game; he could have been mistaken; he could have not known what it feels like to be in that position (very few people do). The possibilities are endless.

On top of this, in a world where nuclear war is imminent, Corbyn's cabinet, the army, parliament, or even members of the public could get hold of that nuclear button without your knowledge, and take control of it. So long as Britain has a nuclear weapon, that deterrent exists. What the man in charge of it says is reasonably unimportant if it's a use as a deterrent that is important to us.

The proof is in the pudding – how have we considered the threat of nuclear weapons before? Did we take Saddam Hussein's word for it that he wouldn't use nuclear weapons, or did we go looking for them, assuming it didn't matter what he said? In the politics of global defence, what matters is military might, not verbal intentions. If you consider someone an enemy, or a potential enemy, your ego might be bigger if you feel they have weaker intentions, but there's no reason to suggest you would ignore their defence capabilities.

WHY ARE WE ALL SO EASILY FOOLED BY PLACEBOS?

I find placebos to be extremely interesting. Whenever I want to talk about some inherent bias or error in our brains, I'll often start talking about placebos as an example. It is one of those areas in which we have clinical evidence that none of us are the smart, rational machines that we think we are.

Many of us like to think that we aren't affected by placebos, but there has yet to be a case of someone being immune. If we have a minor ailment, or a minor pain, whether we like it or not, we are quite open to the suggestion of empty medical sounding procedures, and often affected by them as a method of curing it.

The evidence also suggests, time and again, that we are not only easily fooled by placebos, but that we are incrementally fooled based on the level of the placebo we take. Two sugar pills work better than one, an injection works better than a pill, and yes, fake surgery works better than an injection. And that one isn't easy to test!

This area is extremely interesting because it flies in the face of what we know to be true. Placebos only make sense in two ways, yet they seem to exist in at least four.

Firstly, they make sense as some people invent pain that isn't there – sometimes intentionally, or else psychologically fooling themselves – so placebos explain why these people might feel better, as an imaginary cure might rid you of an imaginary illness.

Secondly, they make sense as human beings are sentient and fallible organic machines, and thus sometimes might have aches or pains that won't last. Thus, it makes sense that a placebo might take credit for ridding you of pain that would have left anyway.

These are both simple ways to explain certain effects that placebos have. They also make sense with the 'more dramatic intervention = more dramatic cure' theory, as our bias can deal better with dissolving the ailment, once a reason for there to be a lack of ailment appears. Similarly, dramatic interventions certainly focus the mind on the intervention itself, thus potentially removing attention from minor, fading ailments in the first place.

But there are two ways in which we struggle to understand and define placebos. Firstly, when people who know about placebos and feel genuine pain are suddenly cured. Again, we can doubt these exist – perhaps they were all either faking it or else had a pain that would have disappeared anyway. That seems unlikely though.

More interestingly, placebos can actually work on reducing real ailments. Stomach ulcers, for instance, can be shown to reduce on the placebo effect.

What does this mean, exactly? Perhaps that there is a psychological basis to these kinds of ailments. Maybe stress, or some other brain state, is creating chemicals in the blood stream which are worsening the state of the ailment, and a placebo/clinical attention of any kind simply soothes the stress. Plausible, but largely unproven as yet.

Either way, this is what makes placebos such an interesting subject of study. They work in obvious situations where you would think they might, and they work on people that you would expect them to. But they also work on all of us, and in situations where you would really doubt that they should have any effect at all.

What I find most annoying is not the lack of interest other people have in placebos, but that many people are keen to attribute real, tested placebo effects to alternative medicines or fake medical cures. The placebo effect shines light on how we humans work, so for people to pass it off as the effect of an actual drug or treatment is disappointing. In some areas, where the placebo effect is shown to be what is going on, such as when people use things like homeopathic treatments, we see people desperate to attribute it to homeopathy rather than the effect we know it to be.

Either this shows people don't really understand what the placebo effect is, or that they wish to exploit it for deceptive purposes. In reality, it could be showing us that we could increase the effectiveness of medical treatments, or prompt a recovery, simply by spending more time on a dramatic/attentive intervention – a longer GP appointment, perhaps. This could be infinitely more effective than issuing repeat prescriptions, week after week, and/or expensive drugs or herbal remedies that don't actually work. There's not a national health service in the world that isn't under financial stress right now, so we need to start lifting these medical quacks out of the landscape, in order for us to use evidence for progress, rather than pursuing the profits of companies peddling nonsense.

SHOULD WE BE PRO-CHOICE OR PRO-LIFE?

Abortion continues to be one of the hottest topics in global politics, if not global culture. Should we be 'pro-choice' and side with a mother's right to abort, or 'pro-life' and side with the rights of the unborn child?

Firstly, let's unpick the idea of 'pro-life'. In US politics that term is a hot potato, but it isn't rationally defined very well. It's incredibly ambiguous, and the word 'life' is used for any foetus at any stage. That's an accurate definition in only one very set, biological method; a foetus (in all but the last few stages or so) is 'alive' in the same way a plant or a cellular bacteria is, in that it grows and thrives in certain situations (ie the womb). More accurate would be to say it is comprised of organic material, not alive in any moral sense that we could consider to be caught by a term like 'pro-life'.

As a result, the debate becomes immediately clearer. Most people's morality tends to draw lines between 'able to suffer/experience life' and 'not able to', rather than 'organically developmental' and 'non-organically developmental'. So, before we've heard any arguments, we've already provided a huge guide as to what 'pro-life' should rationally entail: if we go based on rational conceptions of morality, 'pro-life' could only ever mean 'pro-late-foetus', and thus there is no rational argument to oppose early terminations of pregnancy at all.

That's the rational thing to believe, anyway: pulling a plant up is not inherently harmful, for the same reason that stopping the growth of a few human cells isn't. Just because the cells are forming the early shape of a human baby, and inside a human body, rather than forming a stem and flower from a bulb, doesn't change the principle; if there is no conscious life within that organic compound, it's just an organic compound. And an organic compound is no more able to suffer or experience pain than an inorganic compound. A plant is equal to a rock in terms of suffering, and both are equal to an early foetus. Sentience is the relevant difference, and sentience isn't there until the later stages.

This is why championing the cause of 'pro-choice' is generally important. That organic compound within the womb takes a long time to develop consciousness – and thus to hold sentience. But the woman, whose womb it is, is conscious the whole time. If she is suffering, or being tortured by carrying a baby she doesn't want – or worse still, doesn't want the pain or suffering of child birth – then that is something we should take seriously. And given that we have the medical knowledge to help get those cells out of her, we err greatly by denying her the right to do so.

There's no difference between a foetus in the earlier stages and semen, in rational terms. Cells are cells. So we should be pro-choice in abortion for the same reasons we are pro-choice about whether men want to carry ejaculated semen around in their pocket all day. Sure, give them the choice to carry it around, it might form something meaningful (if you've got an ice pack in there, it might create a baby one day). But, apart from some arguably primitive catholic communities, we don't make men worship their own semen, so we shouldn't make women worship the cells forming inside them either.

Plenty disagree though, which is why this is a hot topic. Unsurprisingly, 'pro-life' people tend not to have rationally formed conceptions of morality. They tend to be from Christian families, or are Sunday church attenders. It's great that we live in a society where people can hold different views, like this. It's just not so great that people *want to* hold them. The use of religion to justify views which cause suffering to women is one of the reasons I oppose religion as a moral matter. I like the saying 'even a blind squirrel finds a nut once in a while'. Religion might lead to some moral decisions, or it might not; it's not a good method of consistent truth finding, as it makes claims based on the beliefs of mythical figures. You can more or less do what you want if you justify it by reference to the will of someone who either doesn't exist, else is conveniently uncontactable, so religious conceptions of morality – especially on abortion – are inherently harmful.

There is of course an important topic in all of this, which starts with the question of 'when does a foetus switch from a set of cells to a conscious individual?' No one has the exact answer to that. We know that the moment an egg merges with a sperm is not it. We know that when it starts to significantly grow isn't it either – we know that you need much more than a few cells, even in fairly complex structures, to have consciousness. It may be that, realistically, some extremely premature babies are not even sentient yet. It's feasible that you can grow organic compounds in various settings without sentience being present, and it might well happen with organically formed pre-humans. If you've seen the episode of House where a premature baby reached out of the mother's womb, in order to grab the doctors thumb, you may be surprised to learn that it is possible, yet not necessarily a sign of sentience. Or certainly not necessarily a sign of advanced sentience; something that could suffer significantly enough to justify forcing a woman to carry them around in her womb, against her will.

It appears sensible to suppose that brains don't just go from 'cells' to 'brain' in a single second of its formation. Rather it's likely a gradual process where it goes from something akin to the organic compound of a growing plant, to something like a very primitive human brain, but without it functioning fully, to something that can experience suffering. It's very possible that a pre-human being could survive in artificial wombs, or on its own in the early stages of life, without any meaningful type of sentience being present. Indeed, an important point to consider is this: doesn't it seem evolutionarily unnecessary for foetuses to be sentient for so long whilst still in the womb?

That statement doesn't provide any meaningful evidence either way, but it does ask that you question your assumptions about at what point foetuses become sentient. Sentience was a necessary development for creatures to better exploit their surroundings, and so to increase the chances of passing on their genes. It seems odd that it would appear too long before birth (though it's sensible to assume it must start to develop at some point before birth). The important issue then becomes a matter of whether the early form of sentience which a baby is experiencing, is really equal to any suffering the mother might have from its growth? Probably not, at least until the very last stages. And even then I'm not convinced.

The case of sentience in foetuses is really something we would need to be discussing with brain development experts, though; people with a background in understanding the philosophy as well as the neuropsychology. Whilst the examples I give are rational possibilities, and interesting to consider, the exact point at which we can say sentience appears is something better informed through neuroscience. However, we can be rationally satisfied that sentience is not present for quite some time after the sperm and egg meet. Thus 'pro-life' is a worrying position for anyone with a desire to have correct moral opinions.

THE MORAL WORRY IN CRIMINAL ALLEGATIONS THAT WE ALL LIKE TO IGNORE

People in Britain, especially, have become rather accustomed to seeing well-known figures dragged in front of courts to answer horrendous allegations. More often than not, it would seem, these are true allegations – for things like child abuse, rape and similar high level, heinous actions. Not only do the media (understandably) enter a frenzied whirlwind at the sight of it, but we all feel a deep distaste for those individuals who are found guilty. These are people who abuse their power in the most sickening manner.

Occasionally – and it does only seem to be occasional, unfortunately – one of these celebrities leaves the process having been found not guilty. More often than not, that's because the accuser backs down, or changes their story in a way which decries the allegation's falsity to start with.

This, too, should leave a distasteful, tainting worry for us. These kinds of cases can often only be tested by victim or witness accounts, as other evidence is hard to come by in those hearings that involve allegations of a sexual nature. We don't often consider that – especially with celebrities who we feel an affinity with or connection to – witness or victim accounts could be reasonably easy to manufacture.

The reason we do not often consider it, and writers don't often write about it, is not because we don't think about it. More likely, it's because we consider it disrespectful to the victims of real crimes for us to talk about it. Of course it isn't: to lie about or manufacture allegations of rape or child abuse is to metaphorically slap the real victims in the face. To attack a person with someone else's suffering is not just disrespectful to those who actually suffer it, but it inherently undermines the scale of suffering, by assuming it's just something we can throw around to attack people with.

This whole issue creates a really tense and difficult process. On the one hand, victims have little evidence to prove their abuse other than their experience. But on the other, perceived experience is a remarkably easy thing to be manufactured: the people callous enough to make up such false allegations would arguably be the ones best at it. Those who lack such a conscience so as to be able to follow through and plan such an allegation from start to finish.

As a result, the media have more or less decided that they have chosen the side of the victim, and so they have ignored this debate altogether. As have well-meaning people who write on all manner of ethics. But of course it's still an important issue. It's difficult to imagine anyone could suffer more than someone who has experienced the physical and mental trauma of these kinds of crimes. A close second though, surely, is the suffering and life-ruining allegations of a false victim, who has falsely imbued someone as a perpetrator of crimes that hold the very highest and most significant stigma in all society.

And we don't need to be comparing levels of suffering, as some shallow utilitarian assessment might want us to, to take both sides seriously. We simply have to retain some sense of sympathy for the falsely accused, and the falsely charged. In an area like paedophilia, for example, these individuals would likely never be able to live down the effect it may have on their lives. They would struggle to ever create meaningful and honest friendships or relationships, forever living under the shadow of something which they have never done.

By retaining the rational clarity which allows for us to sympathise, we at least have a chance of developing a better system. One where victims aren't doubted based on the lack of evidence, but also where false allegations are both ignored and disincentivised. To get to that middle ground must represent somewhat of a holy grail. Who knows if we'll ever get there, short of a remarkable leap in technology. But to even encourage the development of such a system, we must admit there is a problem in the first place.

The victims are not necessarily those whom the courts rule on behalf of, but those who are genuinely wronged, either by a heinous act or an unbalanced process. We must help the courts to better serve victims as a whole.

PREJUDICE OR HEALTH PROMOTION?

I've changed my opinions on most things at one time or another in my life, but very few ethical dilemmas truly have me on the fence. I might change my mind, but it doesn't waver in the middle for very long. On 'fat-shaming', there are areas where I fence-sit like a cat caught between two dog-filled gardens.

Of course, there are huge swathes of arguments on the subject which I spot as rational and fair. As a man of not-slim proportions, it'd be difficult for me not to. I see that there is an irrational prejudice, and unfair treatment, to be found in 'fat-shaming' *per se*. If someone wants to be a certain size, or indeed if someone can't help being a certain size, why should they receive abuse for it? Like any other form of abuse, that aimed at physical constraints such as weight or appearance should be opposed wholeheartedly.

I also see many arguments on the other side. We all pay for healthcare via our taxes, in the UK at least, and given that many forms of obesity are both individually avoidable and draining on our healthcare system, then why should we be silent about people in the 'obese but avoidably so' category?

There are also arguments which are not as strong, yet persuasive. In the anti-'fat-shaming' camp is that of what constitutes 'avoidable'? Any decent and scientific understanding of human life must admit that determinism exists, and so must admit that people are not to blame for being obese – even if it was potentially avoidable – because it is not their fault they had neither the resources nor traits to help avoid it.

The weaker counterargument is one along the same lines. The more studies we have, the more we see that obesity is linked to increased risk of disease and chance of death, and all the misery that goes with it. So if someone can't help being obese, either in terms of resources or personality traits, then we must do all we can do create an environment which helps them avoid it.

Arguably, the kind of environment that is best at helping people avoid obesity would not just tax unhealthy snacks and fatty foods, but also create a societal unacceptance in being obese. Something which creates a look of the irregular about obesity, and which motivates people (albeit with negative stimuli) against being obese. Of course, we currently do this in an entirely unhelpful way – we promote individual rights to unhealthy behaviours, which we defend and protect with our health services, but then also fat-shame to the degree where teenage girls suffer eating disorders such as anorexia and bulimia. These are the real ethical problems with fat-shaming: a society where people are swayed into harmful behaviour with immense psychological and physical suffering.

The argument, of course, goes on and on. What about those people who will never be anything but physically obese? Perhaps because of medical conditions or other completely unavoidable symptoms? Small as that group may be, is it okay to create an environment within society where they have no choice but to suffer?

What about the rights of people to individual liberty? To be as fat or as thin as they like, as healthy or unhealthy as they like – why should they be forced into conformity simply to please someone else's values of what constitutes 'normal'?

On the other hand, we aren't just talking about the selfishness of people, who enthusiastically want to remove the drain which obesity causes to the health care system. We can't provide the system with unlimited funding, and in a society with an increasing elderly population, and all of the complex care needs that go with it, we have a serious funding problem. There are funds that go to helping people who might not be obese had the social acceptance of it been lowered, with whom that same funding could have been used to tackle problems of loneliness or complex illness in the elderly. Perhaps providing care for people with dementia, or other illnesses which we haven't yet researched methods of avoiding.

Thus, whilst fat-shaming is inherently unfair, it seems also inherently unfair that we divert funds from unavoidable illness to treat avoidable illness.

It seems that if there is a solution to this, it is probably found in a middle ground I haven't happened upon yet. Prejudice is wrong, but perhaps there is a way of creating a useful stigma on obesity, which does motivate without causing abuse and negativity toward people who are existing and obese.

Either way, we do know that it is unfair to treat people with stigma, but that it is also unfair to treat avoidable and unavoidable illnesses the same. All other things being equal, people who had no chance to avoid an illness should arguably be given precedent over those who had a chance they did not take; purely as a pragmatic matter of encouraging better future health outcomes. But as we cannot create a fair healthcare system that operates this way – nor a logistically possible one, as individual diseases can often not be *certainly* caused by obesity – then we have a dilemma on our hands, in this theatre of judgement we call society.

DO WE ASK THE WRONG QUESTIONS ABOUT PUBLIC SERVICES?

A couple of years ago, my grandmother suffered a traumatic fall during a night in the care home where she was residing. Unfortunately, it seemed to be the inadvertent switch for the onset of dementia, for which she rapidly hurtled towards after the fall.

As her family, we wondered 'how could this have been allowed to happen?' She had become physically very frail in the preceding months/years, which was part of the reason for her moving to the care home. She had begun to struggle to care for herself, and had some relatively minor falls and accidents. This, rather than a mental deterioration, was the reason for her needing to use social care in this way. So how was the traumatic incident not guarded against? And, having had informal information about the time of the fall and the much later arrival of the ambulance, we also wondered why it took so long for anyone to notice – was there no alarm that my grandmother could have triggered, or monitoring by the care home staff?

A complaint to the care home, and to the Care Qualities Commission that oversee their standards, did little to soothe our concerns. So we also contacted a solicitor, not wanting this to happen again to some other elderly resident. The privately owned care home took over a year to 'hand over' the simple logs about the incident, and – rather fortuitously for the wealthy owners – although we had details of the emergency call, available from the emergency services, the internal door log system was 'not working' on the night in question. So due to a failure in internal systems, no evidence could be provided about how long my grandmother lay on the floor, or at what time she fell.

Prior to the incident, her mental faculties had no doubt been declining – as befalls us all at some stage – but to no huge extent. She now seems to remember little, from day-to-day, since the fall; including not a single memory from the fall itself. She describes the cause of injuries often as being from a fall in the town, or occasionally something more fanciful, with the dementia now regularly merging her everyday life with memories from her younger years. (Along with my grandfather, and later my father, she used to have a market stall in the town centre, so it's common for these memories to come out in her day-to-day life.)

For us, whether causing a leap in dementia or not, it's apparent that the trauma has affected her greatly. Her physical and mental condition has declined significantly. Yet because we have no proof of any wrongdoing, the care home does not have to improve any of its systems, neither is any mark held on its record. This is a little worrying given it took over 12 months for them to post a log which should have been completed on the day of the fall, and that the security systems they have in place were faulty.

The lessons we can learn from this unfortunate situation are simple and most likely replicated up and down the country. Many care homes like this are now privately owned, so there is a common willingness to meet standards without going further than required. There is not only an ability and financial incentive to hide negative facts (for instance, one will not be sanctioned if security equipment is faulty, so one can ensure it is if something bad happens), but also an incentive to avoid any negative assessment which might lead to improved patient care.

This is not rocket science, it's basic logic. Whilst we increasingly seem to live in a conservative world – where everything must be owned and run for profit – it didn't used to be that way, and we had good reason for that. People did used to think that if everything is about profit, then people will run things with the end goal of profit, and the virtue and meaning of things will get lost.

A publicly owned company, for instance, is essentially judged by how well it services the public. The NHS thus rightly has tables about waiting times and diagnoses, etc. But by making the conversation instead about how much it costs, or how much waste it creates, the business interests within politics have slanted the perspective away from public service. They have created a way to turn people against the very services they are in reality supported by, and created a myth that says privatisation is the key. By privatising companies, they argue, we can streamline things to eliminate waste and excess cost.

They forget to mention that what business owners consider waste, and what public services should consider as waste, are two very different things. A safe level of staffing on the night my grandmother suffered her accident, or a back up alarm system, are considered waste by the care home. It can essentially still run without them, and unless it is forced by law to have these things, then it is 'waste'. Yet a system of social care which was run for the benefit of patients would happily include this 'waste', as the goal here is something other than pure profit.

This is by no means an issue which is limited to social care alone. A wasteful post office is one which has stores in rural areas, so privatisation has seen many of them closed. And a wasteful public transport system is one which supports residents in lesser populated areas, so guess which bus stops and train stations get removed?

This isn't the only problem with privatisation. There are two far more fundamental flaws, rationally speaking, namely:

If the business people we sell public services to are so good at eliminating waste and excess costs within companies, why can't they do it whilst the company accounts say 'HM Treasury' rather than 'J. Bloggs' at the top? The need for privatisation assumes the business can only benefit from talent, if talent owns it rather than runs it.

The most perfectly run business in the world will always aim to make a profit – a surplus for security – whilst a public services company doesn't have to. So, all other things equal, a company is logically more efficient when run for public services than for business, as there is more cash to spend.

There are no essays in this book that are a closed case; all are open to new evidence and subsequent change. The goal is not to preach but to get you thinking, playing devil's advocate with your brain. But this is one of a few which I think is as clear cut as they come; we ask entirely the wrong questions about public services, and we have allowed the conversation to become dominated by irrelevances such as waste. It would seem that the longer we allow this, the worse a place our society will become for those who don't own richly rewarding businesses.

HOW FAR SHOULD WE EXPAND ETHICS?

What do we mean by an 'ethical concern'? By the presence of the word 'ethical' rather than 'personal' or 'family', the implication is that ethical concerns refer to the well-being of individuals other than those immediately connected to us.

This is perhaps no shock. When we think of ethical concerns, what comes to mind are social justice and environmental issues: things that could negatively affect groups of other individuals. There is undoubtedly an evolutionary/selfish advantage to such ethical concerns: a safer world for you and your family is a safer world for mine. If you're well fed, you're unlikely to want to attack me and steal my resources. However, when we debate and decide upon ethical concerns, the will seems to be that we're somehow referencing a form of good behaviour or action that is not directly selfish. It often benefits us indirectly, sure, but the direction of the term 'ethical concern', or the study of ethics itself, is outward from our own personal connections. It's about logically expanding ethics, regardless of whether it might put us out a bit. But how far should we expand this concern?

The story of the last two hundred years in the West – if not the story of human civilisation itself – is a tale of expanding ethical concern to rational conclusions. We've gradually moved our legal protections from a few leaders or wealthy barons at the top, seeking out further levels of equality as we go. From the rich to include the poor; the men to include the women; the whites to include everyone else. In most recent years, we have finally also seen some gradual progress from the dominant straight ideology to the full spectrum of gender and sexual preference, or even lack of. All towards a respect of individuals rather than labels.

It would be foolish to claim we're knocking at the door of perfection in any of these areas; our sexist, racist and homophobic tendencies stand strong in most cultures, and influence areas from equal pay all the way through to outright slavery and murder in some parts of the world. However, it would also be foolish to ignore the improvements year on year. The general global progression is upward, however gradual it may seem, and however many setbacks we have.

Whilst we rightly continue to climb upwards, climate change hovers over us as the ethical concern to trump them all. Stopping that crucial 2 degree increase in global temperature is a matter of saving countless lives, as well as stopping the impending future changes, which would cost far more. A steeply sliding scale towards unprecedented further levels of individual suffering.

Yet among our current ethical struggles, and our impending but surely progressive environmental ethics, there lies a sore thumb of an area, which we seem to lack consideration for in any great degree. In this area we imprison and slaughter 60 billion individuals globally every year whilst having the scientific knowledge that they suffer, potentially as much as, if not more than we do. We cause this suffering because it is pleasurable for us to do so, on a very basic level of taste or aesthetic entertainment. Yet we alleviate our guilt not by significantly reducing the numbers used yearly, but by demanding they come labelled differently, or are imprisoned in places with greater space, or given access to a fenced off outside area with which they can occasionally exit their confinement (but never fully leave).

We deny many natural characteristics to these 60 billion individuals, among everything else we do to them, and when we're challenged about it, we react with bizarre claims like 'lions do it' or 'we've always done it' or, even worse, 'I couldn't possibly stop doing it'. I imprison and slaughter 60 billion individuals a year because 'I couldn't *not* do this'. These are not the honest claims of a species with a moral history to be proud of, like ours.

When we hear the arguments about climate change and the impending doom, it forces us to sit up and take notice. After all, we may get to a stage where all 7 billion sentient, life-loving human beings may be at risk of death. This is a huge number. Perhaps by the time it happens there will be 10 billion sentient humans, maybe more. An unimaginable number of people, suffering because we couldn't be bothered, or couldn't get organised, to do very simple things; it's heartbreaking.

Yet right now we kill at least 60 billion non-human, but entirely sentient, animals globally *each year*. That's almost ten times more sentient individuals every year than we seem to worry about climate change affecting. If climate change doesn't strike us significantly for 30 years, that's 1.8 trillion animals we've killed in the meantime. If it doesn't hit us significantly for 50 years, that's 3 trillion. **Three trillion lives.** They might have fur, or walk on four legs, but we've ignored the immense suffering of 3 trillion individuals because of our own badly formed mental gymnastics.

At what point in history will we admit that it's heartbreaking how we already kill unimaginable numbers of less capable sentient individuals, who can do nothing but cluck or oink back at us? At what stage should we give up on our ridiculous excuses which we've been aiming at vegans for the last ten years? At what point do we hold our hands up and admit that we were wrong, and start advocating a move away from this behaviour rather than towards nicer presented forms of the exploitation (as 'free-range' has become)? And why are we all waiting for everyone else to move first?

These are questions which weigh heavy in the rational analysis of animal ethics. Current industry specifications mean that where there is consumer concern for animal welfare, the industry will act to appease it with labels (free-range, freedom food or organic, for example) which do little but attempt to improve a minor aspect of the animal's treatment in a way which is cost-effective for the company. They still live in ill-suited, cost-orientated environments, and they still suffer the indignity and finality of the slaughterhouse. A couple more inches or a thrice-weekly stroll doesn't even chip away at the monument of exploitation we are maintaining.

These improvements are never improvements in any significant sense of the word, and of course they couldn't be. Animal farmers still need to make money, and these are industries already propped up by eye-watering levels of government subsidies – interventionist money that would be deemed obscene in most industries. Real improvement could only be forced by significant drops in sales – in other words, abstention – not merely a murmur of discontent. And given the massive hole in our government spending budget, we could use those subsidy funds elsewhere, too.

I started this article by asking 'how far do we expand ethics?' I've also answered it: we should expand it as much as reason demands, and not allow excuses to stand in the way.

Instead, we currently extend our ethics begrudgingly, only as far as we have to. We wait as long as possible until we act about the inequalities in society, doing the bare minimum until we are pressed. Sometimes it takes marches, sometimes protests, sometimes it takes violence. Occasionally we have to wait for the less progressive generations to die off altogether – as harsh as that sounds – which perhaps explains why women *still* suffer on lower pay for the same jobs as men. This isn't to give up on older generations, but the older we get, the more ingrained into our current lifestyles we generally become. Many people of a certain age are capable of shifting their opinions and making honourable additions to their lifestyles. Most, sadly, don't. But then many of younger ages don't either.

Animals don't protest, or if they do, they do it in solitude, uninten-tionally, by innocently not knowing better; protesting only to those of us who are critically examining our use of them. As a result, they suffer the slowest shift in public perception. Indeed, it's been centuries since Descartes wrongly and religiously dubbed animals as unfeeling ma-chines, yet we've only just gotten to a place where we even deem it acceptable to feel guilt at their treatment. But, hey, maybe that's the tipping point. We expand ethics by pushing ethical concern to its logical conclusions, and that concern usually only begins to accelerate once the guilt sets in.

Those relatively useless labels we talked about earlier – most notably, free-range – arguably do little if anything for the animals, but succeed commercially because they play a role in soothing our guilt. None of us know what they even mean, we just use them to excuse our behaviour. The fact they exist means we can be deceived out of guilt fairly easily. But at least it shows that we do feel guilt; that speaks well of us. And guilt is how we expand ethics. It's not pretty, it's not particularly rational, but it appears to be how society works. Shocking images and farm exposés have been tried and failed – but a gradual growth of guilt, forced by rational argument and realisation, is how we will climb to the next level of ethical thought: animals.

ARE WE WRONG ABOUT TRANSGENDERISM?

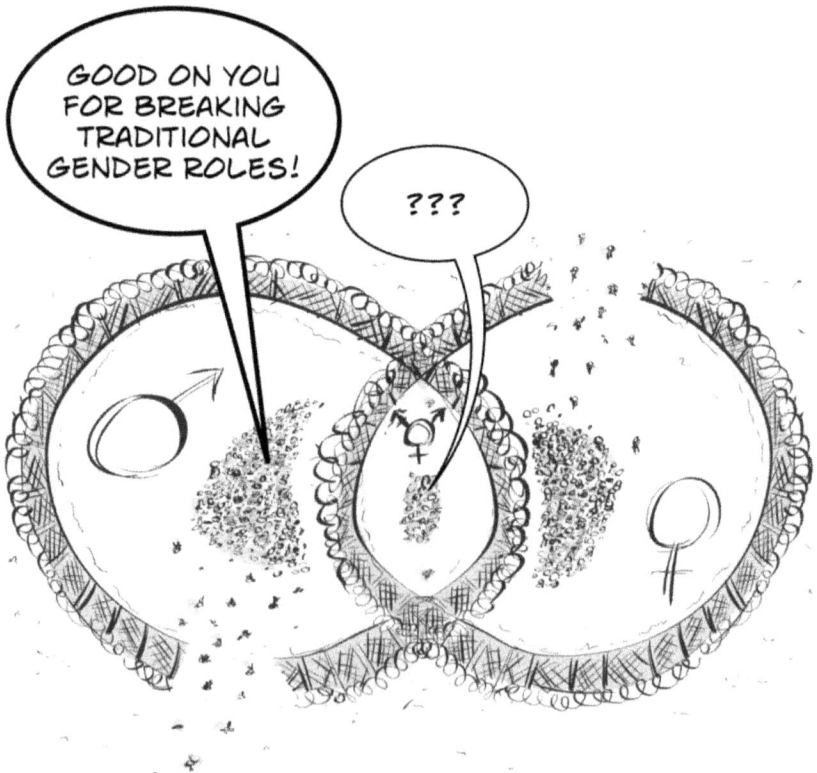

For some time, there has been a strand of radical feminism – among others – that has a problem with transgender people. As the media in many Western countries has grown more tolerant of transgender people, this radical feminist viewpoint becomes harder and harder to hear.

Whilst women and homosexuals were justified in their right to equality, some radical feminists differentiate between these types of movements and transgenderism. They claim that whilst homosexuals have a will to love or be in a relationship with someone of the same sex, transgender people do not deserve the same protection; they are simply a subset of individuals who desire the *social roles* of the opposite gender, rather than any meaningful, actual personality trait or physical characteristic.

At first, this seems to be a very strange argument. The ever-increasing victories of equality campaigners have elevated women, protected homosexuals, and generally fought for the tolerance of people who peacefully reject mainstream behaviour. Why should this tolerance be withheld from people who wish to be treated as the sex opposite to that they were born?

The only rational reason comes in the process of the definitions. By being female, you are simply – physically – not male. To be gay or lesbian is to naturally or socially be attracted to people of the same sex. Similarly, to be bisexual, asexual or pansexual is to have different romantic or sexual desires to the mainstream. These are all about being physically different or wanting different relationships, perhaps being attracted to different mates than most people. But transgenderism instead seems to be about wanting different social roles, or different physical characteristics. Fair enough, that is different. Many men want to be taller or smarter, and many women want bigger breasts or bums, but we don't see these longings as something to be respected and protected as virtuous.

Noting that transgenderism is different in this manner is fine, but that doesn't make it necessarily the same as other forms of longing for physical or characteristic difference. Within the spectrum of transgender individuals, you may have people who feel daily distress and anxiety about the fact that they were born as the wrong sex, or others who feel miserable following the social norms of the sex they were born as. So whilst there may be many transgender people who want to be seen as the opposite sex for shallower reasons of physical longing, desperation to be like celebrity role models, rebellion or – most controversially and very unlikely – to have unrestricted access to unaware people of that sex, you can't tar everyone with that brush.

What's more, the term is so broad that one could be desiring of a complete, reconstructive and hormonal sex change, or else simply enjoy dressing as and playing the social role of the opposite sex. It makes no sense to flatly oppose anything as general as transgenderism when such a spectrum exists.

The important point, surely, is that there are many people within the broad umbrella of transgenderism who do suffer significantly by being forced to be, or play the social roles of, the gender opposite to the one they identify with. The answer then, it would seem, is similar to other cosmetic or social identity issues that humans face.

We don't, for example, generally respect the wishes of young girls to opt in for breast enlargement surgery, but we recognise that in rare cases it can be an identity issue which causes significant suffering, and in those cases we relent on our opposition. Similarly, when people are born with facial birthmarks, they can often live years without it bothering them, only to become hypersensitive and full of anxiety about it in adult life. In those cases we also relent and admit the necessity for physical reconstruction to ease mental suffering. There may be plenty of cases of transgenderism that fit this kind of definition of physical suffering that needs treatment. Perhaps most do.

What is more difficult to justify is the issue of wanting to disregard naturally obligated social roles on their own; the type of transgenderism that longs for the social/cultural norms of the opposite sex. Given that we like to think that we are tolerant of 'feminine' men and 'masculine' women, there is no need to define a rejection of any gender norms as transgenderism; a person should not be forced to fulfil the entire spectrum (or indeed any) of the norms associated with the birth-gender in the first place. If we live in a culture that does not accept this, it is a fight for rational equality – for human individuality - not for transgenderism. Transgenderism is most often seen as the wholesale replacement of one gender with another, whereas if we are arguing that someone's gender shouldn't dictate their norms in the first place, then transgenderism isn't actually part of the same fight. We shouldn't agree with such strict, set norms for males and females in the first place.

The main point on transgenderism, however, continues to be primarily about suffering. If someone wishes to be transgender due to suffering, it makes nothing but sense to allow them the right and the equality to do so. That some people might be transgendered for more shallow or suspicious reasons should be of no more significance than people wanting to have cosmetic surgery for shallow reasons; some people still suffer immensely by not having it, and they matter.

Perhaps there is an issue of miseducation at play here, though. If we are socialising people to believe that they must either fulfil 'male' or 'female' roles, we are erring badly. One can be either, and follow any mixture of social cultures they so wish, as long as it doesn't harm anyone else. Similarly, very few social norms need to be defined as male or female at all. So if a large group of people are wishing to change their social roles from male to female, or vice versa, this should tell us that we're forcing people into sets of norms which they should never have been forced into in the first place. Individuality may be a key to happier human beings, and the suffering of transgender people may be a symptom of a society which hasn't taken this principle seriously enough; both because they desperately want to avoid forced social norms, but also want to embrace this forcing of norms from a different angle.

WHAT ARE MEN'S RIGHTS ACTIVISTS MISSING?

There is a recent trend – one historically rooted in the enlightenment attitude – of critics engaging with and trying to understand the subjects to which they are opposed. I don't just mean that people want to understand a subject before they judge, which is a thankfully more widespread occurrence, but rather that people try to understand why their opposite numbers hold the beliefs they do in order to better critique/reason on the issue.

One area in which I have recently done this is with the largely white, male group who refer to themselves as "men's rights activists". These are people who believe our focus on feminism or women's rights leave men as poor victims, who themselves need activism on their behalf. You know, because only having most of the world leaders, corporate CEOs, media moguls and otherwise influential people on your side is terribly sad.

Primarily an unorganised group, my instinct is to dismiss the immediately ridiculous nature of their arguments. Racism, sexism and just about every other conceivable prejudice in the Western world favours the people who call themselves "MRAs". Yet this group deem the slow creep toward equality as a shot against their own equality. This is, in at least one sense, utterly ridiculous; to decry slowly progressing equality is to forget that other people deserve to be treated with the respect that you are. That doesn't erode your rights – as MRAs often claim – it simply elevates others to your level of equal treatment. The analogous equivalent would be wailing at lifeguards for rescuing other children from drowning, whilst you float happily with your armbands on. Yes, in this analogy you are a petulant child.

I regularly wonder how people come to, seemingly sincerely, hold beliefs like this. It is easy to dismiss them as ridiculous, or ignorant, yet I think there are more rational explanations for why they hold the values that they do. Partly it seems to be about a fear of change, but this happens primarily because of media misinterpretations of what equality actually entails. This in turn is probably a fault of postmodernism, which seems to most often mutilate feminist theory in order to have its bizarre say.

'Postmodern feminism' is utterly irrational, on the other extreme of the scale from the opinion of MRAs. Like MRAs, postmodern feminism is not in any way organised; it represents a huge swathe of opinion on feminism. Its only shared feature seems to be that facts about feminism are 'experiential' rather than evidence-based.

Some of the more classic features of postmodern feminism include the idea that men cannot be feminists, as by being born a man you are automatically to blame for sexism and thus a shill in the whole thing. Your gender essentially gives you a right to a say, else a right to shut up in this version (the astute among you will notice the exact similarities between this version of postmodern feminism and sexism itself).

Another well-travelled feature of postmodernism is the idea of inter-sectionality – a plausible and academic sounding term, which actually claims that all forms of violence and oppression are intimately (almost spiritually) connected, and thus progress in any one area of violence requires an intersectional, conjoined approach to oppression as a whole. As complex as 'intersectionality' sounds, it is actually simplifying all forms of oppression to some sort of basic act of violence which is always essentially the same. Interestingly, postmodernists in this camp usually do appear to recognise that working to stop one particular violent act – say rape, or slavery – can decrease the incident of violence. Yet they do not consider these successful 'one section' interventions as evidence of 'solo-sectionality'. Similarly, no evidence for 'intersectionality', or indeed coherent theory of how one could either prove or disprove it, has ever been put forward.

It is theories of postmodern feminism such as these, which do things like demonising men or over-explaining the simple, which cause the real fear in groups like MRAs. Feminism is a subject which no rational, clear thinking human being could understand and yet still sincerely oppose, but when it is contorted into a complex and impossible to understand postmodern concoction, suddenly it doesn't look so reasonable. And the goals it holds start to look oppressive.

I might go so far as to propose that had I no academic backing in ethics, and were I to be unaware of what feminism actually entails (which is perfectly possible in a world where pop stars are the main proponents, and even they seem confused about it…) then I might sympathise with MRAs. They fear something which feminism doesn't consist of, but it's not because they've imagined it, but rather because they've been misinformed. The faux-academic nonsense which we call postmodernism has taken a hold of feminism in some pretty scary ways, and if it can have some scholars convinced as to its accuracy, it's perhaps no surprise that they have scared the shit out of some men too.

Of course, some men are also just unpleasant. But that will be clearer when we eliminate postmodernism, and all its goals of inconsistency and anti-rationalism, from academic curriculums. If you still oppose feminism when postmodernism is well and truly gone, then 'missing something' is probably a bit optimistic, and 'unpleasant' becomes more accurate.

IS SENTIENCE A SPECTRUM?

In July 2012, a prominent group of scientists – including cognitive neuroscientists and neurophysiologists – gathered at The University of Cambridge to declare that non-human animals are sentient.

This, of course, is nothing but a modern testament to that which has been relatively well known for a while: that consciousness didn't appear when humans evolved, it existed long before that in the evolutionary chain. We can experience suffering and pleasure, and our ability to show signs of it and to spot signs of it in other animals, has forced the Cartesian opinion that animals are unfeeling machines right out of mainstream rational thought.

A commonly held belief that ties into this is shared by many in the public, as well as championed by an increasing number of animal rights groups: sentience is the relevant characteristic in morality, so we owe every sentient animal the same rights as humans in many areas.

I myself have been a proponent of this view. Having grown up on a farm full of chickens, my views were entirely turned around when I learnt about animal ethics. It quickly became obvious, for instance, that if other animals are sentient then there is no excuse for eating them or killing them in any other needless ways. It was quite a change of path for me, yet one that I stuck to over the years.

Part of me has begun to recognise a slight flaw in this belief, though. If we look back on the short articles in this book on consciousness, I hope that it becomes clear that we humans aren't quite who we think we are. Our desire to see ourselves as immaterial individuals within material bodies is largely inaccurate; we have evidence only to suggest that our personality is a highly evolved method of doing a few basic tasks. We've no doubt become smarter and better organised, and done some really impressive things, but we're still essentially that same organic CPU. In this sense, much of what we see ourselves as – some immaterial soul or being, within a physical brain and a body – is little more than a helpful illusion.

This kind of understanding ties right back into sentience. Our sentience is basically a result of our nervous system – stimuli-detecting apparatus – transmitting signals back which are then felt or interpreted by the main software.

This is where I think people go wrong when thinking about sentience, and where the analogy with computers is both useful and yet incorrect. Consider a high end, top of the range, scientific desktop computer – attached to it is all kinds of new-fangled equipment, and it can do everything from measuring room temperature to providing microscopic images. It can merge all the information it gets into smart spreadsheets and graphs, using clever algorithms to make meaning of the data it receives. Next to it sits an old, very simple calculator, which only has buttons for basic tasks like addition and subtraction (nothing like square roots, as you have as standard on today's models).

Those two items are both computers. Yet the wealth of difference is huge. One is capable of getting and merging all kinds of information, and even of essentially 'understanding' the information it receives – it can divide up microscope data and relate it to temperature data, etc. The other is capable of only doing one set of basic tasks.

This must be the type of spectrum with sentience also. If sentience is a product of evolution, which it must be, then cells didn't one day start to mutate in a way which was immediately sentient from a non-sentient base. Of course they didn't, they evolved gradually. The first sub-species of organisms began to be able to react to light, perhaps, and some species became able to move freely to avoid certain light reflecting phenomena – such as approaching potential predators (at this stage all this arguably happened under the sea). It isn't until much later that we would be thinking of a CPU capable of comparing different types of complex information. But, even then, the first organisms that could compare different information would be the equivalent of that calculator – able to tell the difference between a plus and a minus when certain buttons are pressed.

Those species have then evolved further, gradually into beings that could even think about evolution as a process, like us. There is a large gap between naturally evolved, self-aware super computers and basic calculators. And whilst, arguably, the lower processing species are still sentient, it's not clear how they could experience suffering in any way as meaningful as the higher species.

In relation to animal ethics, this is an unimportant topic. Cows, dogs and pigs are incredibly complex super computers. Humans are simply at a different level – we are talking the quantitative difference between a PlayStation 4 (powerful and able to play lots of games and other software) and a scientists' PC (more powerful, and with better data interpretation), if you would like that computer analogy continued. Both of us, to some degree, are sentient and advanced, but still at different levels.

Yet if all our consciousness consists of is a collection of reaction to stimuli – as I have argued earlier in the book – this difference is also important. To destroy a smart, gaming computer is different to destroying a super computer with self-awareness. And to destroy either of those is much different to destroying a very basic, early form of calculator.

This is where our knowledge of animals lacks sorely. We know they are sentient. We also know they have some sort of awareness - some sort of unified presence with which they strive to live, eat and sleep. But do they dread like humans do? Can they suffer in anticipation – one of our worst kinds of fear and suffering? Can they suffer social stigma at the same levels, to lead to depression and loneliness, the kinds of things that our society is beginning to wake up and see as the big harms to human beings?

It really is doubtful, because what we know about consciousness tells us that sentience must exist on a spectrum. It exists in the same way that a computer's digital ability does. So there is every reason to suggest that suffering human beings deserve much more of our concern than other animals.

However, to suggest – as just about every human being I have met in the last ten years has – that our intellectual superiority means we should kill and eat them because we like the feeling on our tongues, is utterly ridiculous. That stimulus on your tongue is just that. Understanding consciousness, sentience and human superiority provides no more reason to continue our horrendous traditions of killing and roasting dead animals than it does for us to roast and eat lesser intelligent, socially isolated humans. If anything, our ability to think it wrong is a complex level we might want to aspire to. In the same way that computers upgrade their operating systems from time to time, we need to upgrade our moral software. Veganism 1.0 is on the horizon, running on the Rational operating system.

I have now run dry all of my computer knowledge.

IS SEPARATING RACES THE BEST WAY TO ATTACK RACISM?

I'm a white man, which means I'm neither the best person to be strategizing anti-racist endeavours, nor have I suffered large amounts of racism in my life time. I did move to Scotland, from England, as a teenager, and thus do know what it feels like to be dismissed in various situations because of where you're born. I know what it's like to have the way you talk mocked, or the way you've been bought up, but I also know that the people who have mostly engaged me like this have been well meaning and generally anti-racist. English white men are not, in general, a persecuted group – indeed, we are about as far from persecution as you can get – and thus my only experience of persecution has been so minor as to be of a different type, if not a different kind, to the more horrid forms of racism.

There are, as far as I can see, only a few ways in which the Scottish hatred of the English and the racist treatment of many other races are similar. One would be that, albeit a different type, it is an occurrence of people picking out irrelevant characteristics to dismiss someone's interests or opinions. A second would be that it can cause the same kind of misery in individuals, even if it doesn't cause the same cultural problems (ie just because the entire race isn't suffering, individuals still can – and suffering is what matters). And a third would be that similar tactics will fail in attempts to solve either.

Whilst the first two are fairly obvious, the third is arguably the most interesting. It's also sort of related to the first: if the problem is people picking out irrelevant and culturally learned differences as a way to dismiss people, then whether it is related to institutionally backed racism, or simply individualised cultural loathing, we have found a similarity which makes certain tactics a bad idea in both.

Imagine, after having been dismissed by a Scottish person for being English, I decided to take the controversial tactic of starting a campaign aimed at unifying the English in Scotland. Imagine I created twitter hashtags, websites, and explicit messages aimed at allowing the English to unify. Imagine, further, that I decided to call the campaign 'English Opinions Matter'.

Part of that is possibly not a terrible idea. Explicitly tempting Scots to think and talk about their cultural bias against the English might be a good idea, but what good would it do to unify English folks into communities, further than we already are? And what good could it do if, when sympathetic Scottish people said, "Sure, but all nationalities' opinions matter too, right?" I rallied against them and argued they were not listening?

This is the rather strange situation we have come to in race-related issues within the US. The horrendous, and often racist, treatment of people of colour across America, often by the police, led to families and friends of victims to create an effective and thought-provoking campaign with the hashtag #blacklivesmatter. The problem is, this campaign went from thought-provoking to bizarre in days.

When well-meaning people – who often weren't black, but sometimes were – did make the point that it is just a campaign tactic to get recognition for the terrible treatment of black people, and of course "all" lives matter, it was shouted down by a postmodern section of the anti-racist movement. This section believes, contrary to the values of the enlightenment, that we shouldn't admit truths if they disagree with our tactics. So rather than striving to force equality for people of all races, they end up making strange statements decrying the truth of ideas like "all lives matter", in an attempt to maintain the same hashtag. Rather than using these ideas as a springboard – taking advantage of the thought-provocation it has succeeded in making – it ends up just trying to stick as an alienating attack against those who have been provoked into thought by it.

Let's analyse this to ensure my argument isn't just the ramblings of a privileged, white, British man. We should, I hope, be able to agree that the point of any protest of racist treatment should be a progress towards more equal treatment, or improved treatment for the race in which the persecution was aimed. So, these campaigns should aim to provoke thought, as well as critical thinking about racism, firstly, and change the opinions of non-black people, secondly. Perhaps, as a third aim, to unify people behind one another's interests, rather than persevering with the idea that we should separate into distinct races at all.

A campaign like #blacklivesmatter would have been a great way to do this, and initially seemed to be. It would provoke thought among white and other non-black people, by equating the word 'black' with 'live', and asking people to think why police officers or others seem to think black lives are somehow less important. It thus has the potential to change minds in those very areas in which it is aimed; black students united with white students on campuses or in streets, holding banners with #black-livesmatter, prompting other white people, who appear to be the main problematic race within the police force, to ask why would people of all races be protesting with this sign if there wasn't something seriously wrong? Finally, then, it also has the ability to unite – not just protestors, but any audience it reaches.

When it got to the stage of media asking, "Isn't it true that all lives matter, though?" the protestors had a perfect chance to begin linking this process to even greater goals. "Yes, of course all lives matter, but America seems to have forgotten that black people are still people." Anything like this, that accepts the questioning truth of those who have been provoked into thought, whilst still creating a strong argument out of the campaign, has just created something that could potentially change the state of society. Indeed, remember Martin Luther King Jr's speech: after concerted campaigns for black rights, he linked black and white children playing together as the goal of the future, and the imagination of a nation, and of a world, was ignited.

Imagine, instead, that Martin Luther King Jr had approached such questions of integration with the kinds of statements that postmodern-ists did after the #blacklivesmatter campaign. Imagine he called anyone who tried to speak about white children racist for not listening to black people alone, and thus not respecting the campaign. Imagine too, if he had dismissed any white person who had campaigned alongside him, and had told him that only black people could talk about racism, and he was wrong by virtue of not being black. It sounds strange – indeed, it's arguable the world would be even less advanced than it is today, had he opted for this tactic – but it's the tactic that many in the postmodern side of the anti-racist movement have taken.

This has led to an almost race-related split, which was kind of the problem in the first place. A white person like me, who has been uncomfortable with discrimination throughout his life, is said to be inherently racist by virtue of the fact that I have the same skin colour as those who so often discriminate against blacks. Similarly, my opinions are said to be worthless if I disagree with a black person, as the colour of my skin means that I am not as qualified to talk about the issue. This seems to be not only an embrace of the poor reasoning that created such a racially divided and harmful society in the first place, but it also seems to be a rejection of enlightenment values itself. If anti-racism is a just cause, and fighting it is a just goal, then words and arguments alone are what matters. Straying from this by ring-fencing opinions from criticism is, in the long run, a tactic which can't possibly bear fruit.

This is the real shocker. In America, especially, politics and the other large institutions seem to be run in such an old-fashioned way, allowing religion and prejudice to rule the entire system. By opposing the establishment with the opposite type of prejudice, you are simply embracing the same rules, the same problems. It's the equivalent of trapping an intruder in your house and then setting fire to it, with you both inside.

What the enlightenment and the rise of reason has shown us, is that rationalism brings reward, and great progress, when we use it to defeat old ways of thinking. People gravitate towards the logical, because that's where we move forwards: people want to be more secure, or better off, and they want to avoid violence. The movement against establishment racism or other types of prejudice is surely best served by creating a persuasive and rational movement that opposes that entire way of thinking.

Dividing people by the colour of their skin is the root problem, second perhaps only to our continuing failure to oust faith and prejudice-based belief systems. To put forward dogmatic prejudice B as a solution to dogmatic prejudice A, is rationally and practically useless. Never, in recorded history, has racism beat racism into equality. It doesn't even make sense.

HOW DO WE ENSURE A NEUTRAL MEDIA?

I'm an ardent supporter of capitalism, albeit a more reformed and fairer version than we currently have in the West; it's been years since anyone like Noam Chomsky had an effect on my views as a writer or a theorist. Yet I maintain there is something bizarre about how we allow the media to function in our free society.

I'm not an anarchist; I'm not really a socialist either. In fact I'm pretty mainstream in my political opinions. I'm not confident that any system other than capitalism could motivate human beings – as conscious biological and psychological organisms – to useful or fair organisation. Among people who hold relatively mainstream opinions like me (though, admittedly, radical compared to many right-wing politicians), criticism of the entire media system is uncommon. My views are modest on economics and politics, but majorly critical of media, and that's relatively rare.

I tell you this so as to assure you that my arguments about the media are of a rational intention rather than an ideological one, whether you agree with them or not.

*****

The function of the media is to inform and provide news to the population. We all have jobs to do, we all have roles to fulfil, and in any democracy we cannot all be involved in or informed of every political decision. Indeed, for society to function when there are millions of us cooperating, we have to put a lot of trust in people to run the political and economic systems for us.

The political side of this, though it has flaws that could be improved throughout, is of the right kind. We have open and fair elections to select our politicians, and we can hold our leaders to account in some ways. The biggest problem I see is with the media: we rely on this to inform us of what decisions our leaders are making, and on neutrally analysing what is going on.

We can't, for instance, know if every economic policy is valuable, successful and/or efficient, just as we can't be involved in every political decision, so we need investigative journalists and media analysts to provide this important role.

If our journalists were just bad at this, that would be one thing. That wouldn't be a systemic problem, but perhaps more of a problem with our talent pool. But several sources do an admirable job. Sources like the Guardian or the Independent provide analysis, and use economic experts, to get news to us. Though, even they often pick out the most sensationalist stories or bizarre opinions to grab an audience.

The problem is more visible with tabloids, or market owned newspapers. We rely on news media to inform us neutrally, otherwise we have little to no check on our politicians, yet many newspapers are owned and influenced by large moguls who have opinions which they can use newspapers to spread. So the vital job of news media is not fulfilled, and instead we end up with unelected moguls and conglomerates that can push their own opinions towards their editorial staff. Biasing our opinions of what the facts are, and what is important.

This isn't a leftist critique of the media but a rationalist critique of the system. A free media is absolutely necessary in a democracy, and must not be a tool of the government, otherwise it fails to be free. But if it then becomes the tool of an individual, or a financial interest, it also fails to be free. Whilst left and right governments alike have done their ideological bests in ensuring the freedom of the press from government, neither has done anything to safeguard its freedom from other large interests.

Partly, this is down to the conservative right's will for everything to be monetized: less regulation and as free trading as possible. Which, of course, will be backed by moguls and companies who have the same will, hence they own large publishing companies to earn money. The liberal left have allowed it from a similar kind of libertarian leaning, becoming obsessed with the 'freedom' of the press, without ever realising it was forgetting that freedom means from bias interests as well as governments.

The problem exists as much today, in the media savvy world of 2017, as it did 20 years ago, when newspapers ruled the roost. The 2015 UK election, for instance, saw right and left divides as usual, but the left support coming largely from the independent Guardian's journalist-led approach, and the right from tabloids and broadsheets with vested interests (which hardly seems fair, given the reliance our population has on media to inform). The resulting imbalance, as it has in almost every election for decades (except for when the political left leaned right), supported the conservative right. The Guardian posted investigative journalism about the manifesto promises, whilst the tabloids posted pictures of leftist leaders eating bacon sandwiches in an ugly manner, or the Scottish National's leader as some sort of dictatorial overlord.

What we are left with is a population of people being informed only by the interests of the people who own newspapers. People able to spin bad news, ignore important topics, and inflate the smallest things – be they pictures of breakfast, or relatively unimportant opinions. It's bizarre. We have such strict rules in politics, but arguably its most important sister – the media – goes completely unchecked in terms of its neutrality.

This is not an Issue of interest solely to those on the left, or to those like me with an explicit interest in politics or economics. This is something deeply unfair and wrong at the heart of society. It's something which means our political system cannot function as it was intended to, something which throws into imbalance all of the theory that supports the idea of democracy in the first place. Democracy doesn't work in large countries full of people if the media doesn't remain neutral and free from government and personal, vested interests. That is an issue which should motivate every human being in society, regardless of political opinion.

THINGS I BELIEVE THAT ARE PROBABLY FALSE

OR

CORRELATIONS I HAVE NOT EXAMINED THE CAUSATION FOR

I may work in ethics, but I have prejudices. Quite a lot, actually. Whilst I endeavour to remove those which evidence or reason shows to be incorrect, there remain many more: some I will be aware of, some I will not. Similarly, some are more important than others (and arguably the more important ones are easier both to see and to get rid of). The following are two honest examples – of varying levels of importance/prejudice – to hopefully spur some thought as to your own. My intention being that by brutally laying out examples of my own lazy thinking, for everyone to read and criticise, you may be more aware of your own.

I can't help but believe...

1) ...that there is a connection between intelligence level and stopping, without forewarning or assumed forethought, in the middle of busy pavements.

Throughout my life, I've always had a respect for other people. I may not enjoy being around them all the time, I may also not enjoy hanging out in busy environments for large amounts of time, but I'm always very aware of the effect my actions are having.

If I was to be walking down a busy street, then realise I had to turn around and go the other way – or even stop to check a message, maybe – my head would immediately start thinking how I can best do this without inconveniencing other people. My thoughts would turn to quickly veering toward the side of the payment, so I am out of people's way, before stopping/turning.

You might think that's a bit obsessive, or that I care too much about what people think, but I'm just trying to be rational and not to put my own interests ahead of others (theirs may well be more important). If I was stopping to get news of a critically ill relative, or turning to run to the hospital for some similar reason, then quite rightly I might decide that my social etiquette goes out of the window. But, in general, my sudden requirement to check my phone or turn around is likely to be no more important than the interests of the 2-6 people behind me who are going to likely run into me, trip over, or otherwise be annoyed if I suddenly and erratically change direction.

Of course my kind of etiquette on pavements is not quite as important as the same behaviour on roads; cars can do much more damage, and cause risks to life if they suddenly break to a halt without warning, or swing around to the other side of the road. My decisions when walking are not as important, yet it's hardly like I'm thinking about much else when I've realised I need to stop walking in one direction; it costs me little to care what the people behind me are thinking.

Finally, no one has ever taught me this behaviour. It's just something I started doing when I was young and presumably developing an under-standing that other people probably think like me. There is always a chance that the person walking behind is in a hurry, or can't stop in time without hurting themselves, or will simply just find my behaviour erratic and rude. These are all reasons, in my opinion, to respect their potential interests when turning around in the middle of the pavement. However, no one ever taught me this – it is a pretty obvious action, in my opinion.

So, given that I think I discovered this etiquette myself – and believe it an obvious thing that many people probably do – it leads me to judge people when they don't do it. Quite often I will be walking along a pavement and someone will simply stop. Sometimes I am in a hurry, sometimes I am not, but I always wonder why this person thinks their need to stop is more important than those of us behind them who want to keep going (assuming, of course, there are not disabilities involved). I almost always just start to assume that they must not be that smart, or be willing to think about things to any kind of deeper level, so assume that – intentional or not – they must not be as intelligent as others.

However, whilst I find this basic reasoning compelling, I am also aware that this isn't the whole story. I know that intelligence, for instance, can be measured in all kinds of different ways, and that everyone who fails to share my etiquette probably is smarter than me in at least some way. But this doesn't change my mind, it simply makes me think it is a little more nuanced than a blanket claim about intelligence; it makes me think they are still less smart, in *some* way, just not *every* way.

Similarly, I often challenge my thought that this kind of respect for other's interests has anything to do with intelligence at all. Whilst I think you do need to be capable of thinking about things other than yourself, I think everyone more or less is that capable. However maybe they've just never been prompted. No one ever taught me this etiquette, something must have prompted it. But, still, I meet this challenge with the simple acceptance of a general deterministic nature of human behaviour: sure, people don't act randomly or directly in line with how their mental abilities say they should or could act, but I think it is at least more likely that a smarter person would think about other people's interests – however small –when turning in the street.

So, I conclude, that this is one of the few moments in life when I actually accept that I may have an examined prejudice. Unlike the kinds of explicit prejudice – like racism or sexism – it can't be proved completely arbitrary, and so can't be rationally deduced as a prejudice, but it does seem more likely than many other beliefs I have. After all, even a less generalising view of intelligence, and a less optimistic connecting of intelligence with respect, still leaves me believing a very strange thing. It might turn out that I'm right: one day scientists with too much time on their hands might get a copy of this book and begin correlating random acts of pavement turning with lesser reasoning ability. But even then, my frustration stemming from the previously thought prejudice would still be inappropriate, as people don't choose their reasoning ability.

2) ...that there is a correlation of some sort between drug misuse and wearing sports clothes for non-sports events outside of the house.

Having spent a fair time working in a General Practice (with a high deprivation population and neighbouring pharmacy), and living across the road from another pharmacy, I encounter drug addicts on a daily basis. The UK has a variety of programs for drug addict rehabilitation, and as a result, many GP visits are made by drug addicts, as are many pharmacy visits, where patients receive drug misuse treatments.

At first I was very aware of my developing prejudice about the way they dressed. It can be intimidating when you are first around addicted users of class A drugs, and you notice things you wouldn't necessarily notice of other people. So when I began to notice the same sports clothes on each one it was perhaps unsurprising. Male or female, all seemed to where sports trousers – the types with stripes – often accompanied by a sports sweatshirt, t-shirt or hoody. Often a baseball cap too.

My intention is not to suddenly drop sales of sports brands for non-sports purposes, but this initial prejudice has grown into quite a strongly held believe. People hanging outside the pharmacy are always dressed like this. I do not recall a single time when they wore something different (except for the occasional large coat or jacket over the top – I do live in cold Aberdeen). Similarly, the patients with the slurred speech and vacant look, picking up items like methadone prescriptions, always – without fail – seem to wear these clothes too.

Again, this isn't a completely unexamined prejudice. I haven't tied it as causation, necessarily, and I don't think that the sports clothes shops are supplying drugs with their clothes. Far from it. I think certain under-cultures in society form more than just one general trait. So everyone in a certain drug taking culture may not just take the drug, they may also begin dressing similarly, so as to conform to the same kinds of social norms that the rest of us do: when at work we wear black trousers/skirts, and 'smart' tops. In a culture of illegal drug taking, people wear sports clothes.

My prejudice does not – I don't think – spread too unreasonably. I don't believe that everyone who wears sports clothes outside of the house is an illegal drug user. People playing sports often do, as well. But the only other group who wear sports clothes regularly outside of the house tend to be students, and even this group is known for a higher than average population of drug users…

Again, I don't honestly believe it's a matter of causation. And I don't think that everyone who ever wears sports clothes out of the house, for non-sports purposes, is an illegal drugs user. I just think that if you mapped people who did wear sports clothes on a graph, there would be a correlation with drug use.

I'm not even sure that this is necessarily a prejudice. But I am aware that it might be one, and as such it forever remains in my head as something I might just need to uproot and cast aside. Similarly, it arguably does little harm – my judgement of regular drugs users as patients who need treatment, or else unintentional addicts, is more sympathetic than most, due to my experience in the world of medicine. But I'm still aware that judging people at all is not right, and that stereo-types should be cast aside as soon as evidence presents itself. At the same time, I'm not sure it's the best use of a social scientist's time.

DO ANALOGIES WORK?

"GO TO HELL THEY SAID, IT'LL BE HOT THEY SAID..."

Physics, chemistry, and the other 'hard sciences' tend to use physical experiments to collect data and evidence. This evidence allows for theories to be proved right, for hypothesis to be tested, and for the subject to progress. Classically, this has left the less 'hard' subjects in a difficult position, as if they are making claims which can't be physically tested, then how are things shown to be right/wrong? How does the subject progress?

In philosophy – as in economics and various other subjects – we often use the idea of 'thought experiments', as although we cannot physically test, we can posit whether an idea sits comfortably with our other knowledge. A great example is the 'tele-transporter machine', as put forward by the philosopher Derek Parfit.

Imagine a 'tele-transporter machine', which copies and recreates your entire body, atom by atom, millions of miles away, instantaneously. Here we are dealing with a technology that doesn't exist, yet with ideas which do: bodies do consist of atoms, and theoretically nothing more than atoms, so if you could copy and recreate atoms in this manner, then you could theoretically 'tele-transport' a human being.

Consider that you enter one of these machines, perhaps as a transporter to Mars. You walk in to a machine on Earth, and within seconds you walk out of a machine on Mars. Completely unaware of the process you have just been through, you would stand on Mars, perhaps looking back at and in awe of the technology we now possess.

Now, philosophy wouldn't be philosophy unless it made your brain hurt, so consider a second version of that thought experiment, but with a slightly tweaked machine. Imagine that it still copied you atom by atom, but it no longer transported you immediately (perhaps this company has overheads that limit its data transmission speed within the solar system!). Imagine, instead, that you walk back out of the machine on Earth, already copied, and go and sit down in the waiting room. Ten minutes later, you are recreated on Mars, whilst you still sit in the waiting room. They then bring you back in to kill you. Do you see the problem philosophy has caused yet?

What this thought experiment could be used to argue is that if we can perfectly replicate a human being, but not destroy the original, then we have perfectly cloned someone rather than transported them. So isn't there something more than the physical that makes a human being? I mean, the person on Mars thinks they are you, but the person in the waiting room also thinks that. The Martian is exactly physically and mentally the same, but simply isn't you. You don't exist within her body, you don't see what she sees, you don't even smell the fresh Mars air (there's lots of Sulphur deposits apparently, so maybe that's a good thing).

This forms part of the problem of consciousness. We can't seem to explain it via the wholly physical, as examples like the above stop us. If it was wholly physical, why wouldn't the Earth human experience what the Mars human experiences? The next two articles delve further into consciousness, so as not to keep you on tenterhooks, but we shouldn't stray too far from the subject of this one – do analogies work?

Well, what the above experiment shows is that thought experiments are necessary and helpful. They pose questions by positing situations we couldn't otherwise test, and we can use logic – including the total of our knowledge that we've gained from our current world – to explore and solve the problems.

This is exactly the same role that analogy is meant to play. A thought experiment posits an entire, plausible sounding situation that we must either solve, else can use as a third situation in which we can disprove a theory which our current experience otherwise supports. An analogy, on the other hand, tends to simplify an otherwise very complicated situation in order to isolate the variables.

This isolation of the variables through analogy is incredibly important. In the hard sciences, we can often concoct a situation in a lab where only the planned experiment can possibly be affecting the results – the outdoor environment can be locked out, equipment can be sterilised, and human bias/intervention can be all but eliminated. Analogies allow us to isolate variables in the same way within other academic areas, where the world doesn't allow for such physical isolation.

The problem, of course, is that analogies can be misleading. In a lab you can test very direct experiments, so it would be obvious if, say, the wrong chemicals were being used, or the wrong reaction had been forced. Things aren't so clear in analogies. An analogy can intend to simplify a complex situation, but can also fail.

This, however, is easily solvable. We simply need to be rigorous in our analysis of the analogy itself, prior to accepting its results. In economics, for example, there are a huge range of variables affecting outcomes, so there is the potential that any analogy might erase potentially significant affects. But even here analogy is still extremely useful, as regardless of other effects, it is incredibly useful to know what exact effect that one event might have on its own.

This kind of knowledge has led to understanding that government economic stimulation helps economies during depressions, for example, when previously we might have defaulted to a position that we should save government funds during a recession. Evidence has now proved that theory – known as Keynesian economics – to be more or less accurate.

Finally, analogies might also suffer from an increase in bias: people who lack evidence for their theory might use analogies to gain, as it allows a person to peruse the depths of human experience to find a roughly similar situation to support their case. This can be confusing, of course, especially if it is not your specialist area. But learning about the subject in question – looking at evidence that does exist – or analysing an analogy will almost always bear fruit. Any method – whether it be physical or not – should be analysed and criticised if necessary, and that we should do this with analogies does not mean they provide no benefit.

In politics, morality, economics, and many of those areas where human suffering is most reliant, we need analogies to present logical progress and to stride forwards. We need to use them wisely, and to interject when they are used unwisely. But without them we are bereft of valuable experiments.

IS CONSCIOUSNESS MYSTERIOUS?

What is consciousness, or how does it exist? Many people see this as one of the great unsolved mysteries of academia.

We can theorise, for example, how organisms come to be able to react to stimuli, but we often aren't quite satisfied with how they become a 'someone' rather than a 'something'. In other words, we have explained action and reaction, but not solved the problem of 'experience' or consciousness.

I don't quite share in this belief of consciousness being a great mystery. More than anything, it seems borne of anthropocentrism rather than a genuine lack of understanding. If we can theorise how organisms become able to scuttle out of sunlight, or close flowers on top of prey, then it seems very simple to explain how and why consciousness exists: as an even better method of ensuring survival of your genes. Organisms that could experience suffering or other states were very effective at living longer lives, and thus were more likely to survive. This ability to react isn't the only factor in reproduction, but it explains why a wealth of conscious animals now exist.

The element of mystery appears when people assume that consciousness is something more than a process of reaction to stimuli. The assumption is that by experiencing life – by being the same, single person each and every day of your life – you have a unified, mysterious and non-physical 'consciousness' which defines who you are. This great concoction of knowing I am me, or at least knowing that I am more than a collection of reactions, argues that we should believe consciousness to be more than a process of reaction to stimuli.

I think that is a grandiosely mistaken view: things like our emotions and mental states can exist, and we can remember them as a part of a huge personality and ego that our brain has created – we can even develop and change over time, as people – but that doesn't mean that there simply is something immaterial and special about us. This whole thing that we call consciousness is still reducible and explainable with reference to our brains only. Nothing that we can do appears to require anything more than the explanation that we are a well-evolved set of genes, able to effectively pass on our blueprints through the next

103

generation. It is evolutionarily useful that you think you are you, so as to avoid dangers and increase your chances of reproduction, but it is nothing more.

What's more, there is compelling proof of this all around us. If evolution as a description of how life came to exist isn't enough, just look at diseases of the brain. The brain can be injured or diseased in such a way that it could affect your personality, your memories, your experience, your suffering, your happiness, or even wipe out entire portions of your life in the case of severe dementia. Changes to our brains can affect every single thing that we deem makes our consciousness unique and mysterious, from our unified psychological presence to our constant personality. This provides all the evidence we need to show that consciousness is simply a brain trying its best to tie all of these reactions together, in a way that effectively aids maintenance and reproduction (at a basic level).

With reference to modern life, it has also allowed us to evolve a complex reasoning ability, making us so evolutionarily successful that we can actively choose to hamper our ability to live or reproduce.

It is difficult to think about consciousness as what it really is: nothing more than a collection of reactions to stimuli, or lack of stimuli, being brought together and powering a smart CPU-like brain. It's difficult precisely because it is *us* – the people investigating it – that are the conscious ones. However, were we to look at cats or dogs in isolation, given the knowledge we currently have, we could happily theorise and come to the conclusion that consciousness is a collection of reactions. Reactions that create complex methods of avoiding or causing events to happen. But it is not so easy to see that when we have an inflated view of ourselves as mysteriously intelligent and miraculous individuals, rather than as collections of genes.

I certainly don't think this creates any ethical reason to treat each other as collections of genes, though: consciousness has allowed us to be able to educate these magnificent organic CPUs in our heads, to work out how other things work and solve problems in the universe. It has allowed us to be unified presences in the universe, who can suffer or enjoy life; to wait in anticipation of the future, or dread what happens next. We truly are, in this sense, the universe's way of understanding itself, and it's wonderful. If it helps for us to see ourselves as more than organic machines for gene reproduction, that's great. In many ways we are. There's just nothing mysterious about the way we are. And there is no reason that a lack of mystery should mean that we find less meaning in life, or that it makes us less responsible for our actions; after all, consciousness has evolved such that we were able to find meaning or be responsible. Why not utilise it.

In the last chapter, I delved, very briefly, into Parfit's 'tele-transporter machine'. How do we square such a naturalistic view of consciousness with that thought experiment? Reasonably easily, as it turns out. To be 'tele-transported' is simply to be cloned elsewhere. That you don't experience the life of the clone (who is elsewhere) provides no challenge to our naturalistic view of human consciousness, given that we've already established that you are nothing more than a smart CPU. After all, cloning a CPU doesn't make it the same CPU either.

The challenge Parfit really faces us with is to ask what really makes you, you? Even if you were completely physically replaced in the exact same spot, in an instant, you arguably would have died, though the clone and any none-the-wiser friends and family would not recognise such an argument. To them, there has been no more murder than when a comatose man wakes to kill off his previous self. This, in my opinion, is simply further evidence that what we see as our mysterious consciousness or individuality is nothing of the sort; from one day to the next you are arguably not the same person. What matters to others, and what matters to your future self, is how you act, what you do and how you present yourself. You could one day be replaced with an exact replica, and even the resulting replica of you could be completely unaware it has happened. As thought experiments go, this is fairly strong support for the idea that our consciousness is entirely explainable by natural phenomena, and is not mysterious in any way other than we cannot currently technologically create it. This is down only to its complexity, not to some other mysterious or non-physical trait.

CAN COMPUTERS BECOME CONSCIOUS? AND SHOULD WE BE WORRIED?

In the very last piece I discussed what consciousness actually is, which is important in relation to this question, as one has to do away with the myths and big grandiose views of human consciousness in order to get a clear answer.

Human consciousness is a particularly advanced method of collating reactions to stimuli, which is capable enough to calculate abstract concepts and to be self-aware. By self-aware, we essentially mean that it knows of its own existence (or rather, *we* know of *our* own existence); it can learn to judge when it is in danger, and tell when it is being gestured toward, etc.

It's important to point out that we don't quite look at computer 'reactions' in the same way. We have a different language for talking about IT, and so when we talk about computers we aren't quite talking about 'instincts' or 'genes' but rather 'code' or 'programmes'. Thus we actually need to find a way to compare human and computer brains in order for us to judge whether or not one is capable of doing what the other can. And with consciousness, this is of course what we are asking: can computers be conscious, like humans are?

So, let's go back to the start and define our terms a little more helpfully. In the last piece I did note that human brains are analogous to organic, smart CPUs, and this seems to be a fair sentiment. Human beings never make decisions entirely randomly. Instead they make decisions based on things that have happened previously, or things they are genetically predisposed towards, one way or the other. In this sense, our brains are heavily deterministic. Given the exact same situation again – if history were to repeat itself exactly – we would always choose the same answer.

So, in order to accurately compare human and computer 'brains', we simply need to identify what the basic 'root code' is for human beings. Or, in other words, what are we built/evolved to do, for which all of our more advanced programming is an effort to assist with?

Evolution provides us the answer for this. Our bodies and brains are evolved to pass on the genetic blueprints to the next generation. So our brains have primarily become coded to help us do a few primary things:

maintain our own lives, protect relatives/social colleagues, and repro-duce. Our programming on top of this – our desires, instincts, abstract capabilities etc – all stem from that root code.

Computers, of course, are coded to do whatever we wish. So, if we were to code them to have the same (or similar) basic root code that we have – a selfish set of primary goals – then there is some suggestion that they could well become conscious to the level that we are, given the same processing capabilities. If they had the same computational abilities, and the same root code, there is no reason why they could not have similar thoughts and patterns of behaviour to us. The difficulty, of course, lies in the detail: human brains were never 'coded', we evolved from animals and organisms of all kinds. There are leftovers from these days, as well as influences along the way, and pinning down exactly what our root code looks like – or to what degree we value one thing over another, or how much genetics affect this – is a vastly difficult task which we are not near to completing. We have not been regularly and inten-tionally 'patched' with updates and software, like a computer is, but rather we have been almost randomly 'updated' throughout the history of our genetic relatives. Some code has been replaced as it wasn't useful, other code has disappeared because it was connected to things that weren't useful, whilst many other things have stuck around because it helped survival, social success or just because it's a side effect of some-thing else that was useful or at least not harmful. We are each a hodge-podge of reasonably successful, but fairly unintentional, natural coding. That's a difficult thing to replicate artificially.

This still leaves a really interesting point to discuss, though. One might argue that if a computer has the ability of a human brain, and the same root code, what is to say a computer could not do things better, and thus make different decisions? This is of course a valid point: two humans at different sides of the IQ scale would play a game of chess very differently, so a smarter computer would likely do so too. They *already* play chess better than us, in fact. If they are given the same root code on any given task, but have a greater computational ability, they will make more rationally capable decisions. It goes without saying.

In turn, this kind of thought has led people to hypothesise that we should be scared if computers get this smart: after all, they will be able to make better decisions than us, potentially willing and able to fight and win wars against us.

This seems rather short-sighted, in several respects. Firstly, even if they have the same root code as us, somewhere in there will be a fair few moral goals. Especially if their root code included any kind of empathy, which we have a lot of. The more rational and secular human society has become, the less wars and violence we have seen. There is every reason to believe the same would happen if smarter, capable computers came along.

Secondly, not only are we many years away from the kind of intelligence that could create self-aware machines at human consciousness levels, but we also have total control over amending root code if problems occur. We could, for instance, create the same smart robots but with a root code that forever placed 'human servitude' above 'self or other robot preservation'. We have spent millions of years organically evolving to a place where we now have animals (humans) that can oppose and avoid their genetic 'root code' to reproduce. But they tend to do so by appealing to another part of the 'root code', to do with ethics, comfort or laziness. These are not rational, universally appealing methods of behaviour; they are genetically imprinted desires which fight for supremacy within us. If computers are built without a root desire to reproduce or reserve energy, then it is not clear how they logically could attain it. The number of humans who turn to genocide or want to become dictators – even with it being a distinct possibility due to our aggressive genes – are small. So with root code manually and carefully programmed, it seems implausible to suggest robots might ever just begin to value the idea of genocide or power for no good reason.

Similarly, if we are worried that one day there might be robots that could wipe out humankind, there is the same level of worry that we one day will create a computer game that wipes out all computer systems. Yet we are capable of not only defending against this risk (with things like anti-virus software) but we also tend to build code in the first place which has a point rather than is purposefully destructive. The rebels who do not code kindly encounter our defences, and rarely get further than an occasional hacking. Similarly, the type of robot that had the ability to cause great, unstoppable genocide, would need the kind of evolution and work on the code such that huge resources would need to be ploughed into it. And it isn't plausible that such destructive groups have this kind of resource, whilst civilised sources don't have the ability to code technology (robots that combat it themselves) to defend against it.

This argument of fear of Artificial Intelligence is persuasive because it points to our own human problems, whilst playing on our fears about the acceleration of technological know-how. But we have to remember that we have no way of reprogramming human beings. We have become an undoubtedly destructive species, by any scale, and that worries us because we wonder what smarter people with the same flaws would do. So when we ponder robots, we suddenly get very nervous. But for the same reason that we shouldn't necessarily worry about smarter aliens, smarter computers pose even smaller problems. Humans can't be reprogrammed easily, but robots can. Humans can't be put into isolation to have their brain's basic code altered... not yet anyway... but robots, even now, can. Compared to smart robots, humans are a vastly more dangerous proposition as they are less predictable; they have wildly differing 'root code'; all kinds of instinctual weaknesses; built in desires to be lazy and ignorant; and an organically created code which is impossible to amend. If robots were to become problematic, they could doubtful reach this level of danger.

But this leaves one tiny caveat, a further hole in the logic which might leave cause for concern: what if robots became smart enough to amend their own root code?

As much as this seems to be a sensible criticism, it seems highly speculative. After all, if smart robots had been developed, and they were capable and conscious like human beings, the root code would be its very highest guide of how to act. They would underpin much of its secondary and tertiary beliefs and desires. Thus it's not clear how the desire to change one's own root code could really occur (if it was physically possible, that is).

This is where analogies with humans break down, and not just because we cannot adjust our own code. We cannot, I don't think, fathom what it is like to have the ability to do so, and we can also not fathom what it is like for our own 'root code' to be hard wired. As I mentioned earlier, we evolved everything we are very gradually, with many conflicts and problems along the way. And whilst our DNA is hardwired, our mental code probably isn't coded to be quite so fixed: people do become murderers, some people kill their own children, and some are completely asexual. Our primary code can be genetically altered away, as well as experientially reduced throughout our life. It's not clear that a robot's could be.

So although we can theorise being a person who is unsatisfied with the way we are in some fundamental way, and being willing to experiment with changing our root code, we should also be aware that this could only really be the case if we became genetically or experientially removed, to some degree, from those basic instincts. I'm not clear on how computers could get like this as their root code is not organically formed, but hard wired. Even if it developed the ability to change its root code, it seems unlikely that it would, or could.

This is the one part that leaves room for concern. But, as I stated earlier, there are a plethora of safety techniques which could stop any problems before this occurred: the equivalent of anti-virus checks and software, not to mention the addition of code that could stop a will to change one's own root code. Perhaps even smart computers that are built specifically to find root codes that have been changed, or codes that provide danger. With advanced technology comes new danger, but also the greatly increased ability to protect ourselves with that new technology.

I think it's perfectly reasonable to suggest that computers could become conscious, when we look at what consciousness actually is. And though there are some theoretical caveats – far, far into the future, which will probably be solved by practical experiment and application – I don't think there is a great deal to be concerned about.

PARADOXES PROBABLY DON'T EXIST

Space is infinite. Yet something cannot go on forever, else it lacks the physical constraints necessary to be 'space' in the first place. For it to exist, it must stop, or end, somewhere. Nothing can go on forever, everything must be caused and thus have a beginning and end. But if it does have an end, what is on the other side? And on the other side of that? It is paradoxical to consider, but space must both be finite in having an end, and infinite in terms of forever having something 'outside' of it (which also must be defined as 'space' to some degree).

This is an illustration of the philosophical term 'paradox', where something has two seemingly conflicting yet logically necessary states of being.

There is no doubt that paradoxes do exist in our current knowledge: there are plenty of things we understand, at current, to be paradoxes. Take the study of quantum physics. It deals with the study of the very smallest pieces of matter in the universe. But, however small you get, something else logically must make up that 'thing'. Atoms contain electrons, which orbit a nucleus, which is made of protons and neutrons, which are made of quarks, up quarks and down quarks etc. The better your ability to magnify that which you are looking at, the more precision you will be capable of, and, as a result, the lower the level of make-up which you can observe and define.

This both creates somewhat of a paradox, but also solves one. It creates one in the sense that this must go on forever, as far as we understand; even if we were to start theorising that the next level down is purely energy – whatever that means – how does that work, and what's that made up of?

This certainly is no lesson in theoretical physics, as I am not in a position to provide one. But on a very basic level, it solves one of the more obvious paradoxes in theoretical physics. Within quantum mechanics, there is often talk of extremely obscure and/or fantastical theories, that physicists posit as necessary to explain how this small level of matter (which seems to react differently to normal physics) is connected to the better-known rules of physics (general relativity, gravity etc). They note that atoms respond in bizarre ways, often appearing in two places at once, which is a paradox, as something cannot be in two places at once. Trying to marry this basically observed behaviour with normal physical reality, means physicists have come up with all manner of odd theories – from the hypothesis-weak string theory to the blatant mysterious 'multiverse', in which there are many 'universes' on different plains.

Yet – simply put – when we know there is always a lower level of activity in the physical world that we can't observe or as yet understand, there is always reason to believe we are missing something important. To try to tie in the documented and bizarre behaviour of atoms with the rules of larger physics, on a basic level – as if to say these are the two fundamental worlds we must theorise together – is missing the other aspects we cannot yet see. It's like trying to theorise a Victoria sponge cake by using just the ingredients of the bottom and top halves of sponge, ignoring the cream and jam in the middle, as you lost that part of the recipe. Whatever sound method of baking you use, you're ignoring vital elements in its make-up. The result will look similar to a Victoria sponge cake, but with one half floating above the other, and no seeming connection between them. You get a counter-intuitive result, but we would expect you to if you're missing a vital cause of the situation you are trying to replicate. Your new look Victoria sponge does not disprove the traditional one, you've just missed something.

The Victoria sponge – appetising as it is, in baking and theoretical physics – is a great link to the evidence-based problem with paradoxes. If paradoxes did exist, like other components of logic and scientific validity, it would be very strange that we have never experienced them in the larger world, where we could observe it more easily. We experience logical consistency on a daily basis – we can concoct laws, test them, and use them to create unimaginably advanced pieces of technology, which humans even 100 years ago would have marvelled at. You don't create supercomputers, earthquake-resistant buildings and rockets capable of flying to the moon and back, without a reasonably sound grasp of logic and how thing work. So, how strange that things never just 'don't work' for reasons of paradox. How strange that when things don't work, we can find the logical reason why, and it not be because the items we work with have a severe paradoxical nature. And how strange that if we fix the problem, things then seem to work. Even when the greatest of ideas fail, we've yet to see evidence that it was because of some mysterious paradox in its function.

When it comes to theories about the very large, like the nature of the universe, or the very small, like in quantum physics, that is the most likely place you would identify paradoxes, as it is exploring the unknown. That is where we are at the limits of technology, where our understanding is breaking new borders. We haven't yet formed fixed and tested laws, and we see things that seem counter-intuitive, almost certainly because we cannot see what is causing the odd behaviour. The same paradox exists for everyone, at some point or another, when they put together a piece of flat pack furniture, or wire a plug that seems perfectly done, yet doesn't work: something is missing, we just don't know what. When we figure it out, we'll know, but until then is it really a paradox, or is it just unknown? Paradoxes exist no more for your non-electricians who can't get the plug to work than it does for your physicists who can't link quantum mechanics with general relativity.

We should use the term paradox almost like we use the term 'randomness': to describe things we don't yet know about the causation or the reality. But what we mustn't do is get caught believing that paradoxes are a true nature of anything. To believe paradoxes actually exist – as opposed to believing they are simply a tool of human reasoning, to define that which seems counter-intuitive to our current understanding – is to believe in the mysterious. But it is also to suspend or ignore the great wealth of understanding we have on issues that we do grasp, and have explored more fully. Car engines don't suddenly stop for no reason, they stop because of mechanical breakdowns. Rain doesn't randomly fall; it is a result of various environmental events and cycles. All the evidence we have says that when we more fully explore any given subject – and gain the necessary level of understanding – we come up with rational explanations that follow a cause and effect pattern. Only when we are struggling at the edges of science do we uncover paradoxes, and they are solved when further evidence is observed or better technology is developed.

Paradoxes are nothing but a tool for noting our lack of understanding at any given point. Anything else is ignorance, or an arrogant will to impose human-created mysticism on science.

As I've noted all along, this is especially relevant in modern physics, where physicists seem to be increasingly throwing out their experience of logic and reality, in favour of concocting increasingly mystical sounding theories to explain behaviour for which they simply don't know the causation of as yet. They are ignoring their lack of causal knowledge and instead creating media-friendly mysticism, taking shots at causal theories which look better placed in sci-fi movies than in sensible science. And they are doing it because they are assuming a paradox does fundamentally contradict the current laws of physics.

Is the seeming appearance of atoms in two places at once down to something we haven't yet uncovered about the make-up of atoms – or the smaller components of the space around them – or is it because there are many worlds, so we are seeing the same atom from more than one universe? It's right for physicists to create hypothesis and to test a variety of possibilities, but is the 'many worlds' idea any better than saying 'just because God did it'? We allow hypothesis making to become absurd, in ways which our entire wealth of scientific laws and understanding completely oppose, by allowing ourselves to believe paradoxes exist.

It isn't just physics, either. Medicine suffers a similar problem with many alternative medicines – especially with practitioners who continue to prescribe therapies which are experimentally shown, time and time again, to be placebos. They believe they must work despite being demonstrably shown not to. The belief in ideas like paradoxes has far reaching effects in allowing otherwise scientifically minded people to believe in things which are demonstrably untrue or logically invalid. Perhaps, indeed, the solution is in providing a better logical grounding for students of all subjects, and all ages; a will to solve paradoxes rather the follow them. As people, we can begin by more expressly understanding and debating what paradoxes really are.

DOES THE SUBJECTIVE NATURE OF ETHICS DOOM RATIONAL GOVERNMENT AND ECONOMICS?

In 2013 I released a book called *Rational Morality*, which is due for re-release next year as *The Great Failure of Moral Philosophy*. The intention behind it was not just a layman's guide to rationally assessing ethics – which are so often tied up in things we get taught, but never fully consider – but also to start a theory that could underpin significant social change.

The reason for that last sentence was two-fold. Firstly, as current theories of morality are heavily philosophical or else theological in nature, I proposed that a rational, explainable theory of ethics would be better at motivating people. Which itself comes from the idea that people stick better to acting in a manner they agree with and understand, rather than those rules they are simply told to follow. The best way of achieving change is people wanting and working towards it. If you've ever managed a business, this part of change management – bringing people with you on the change, rather than dragging them kicking and screaming with some disciplined rules – will be obvious to you.

Secondly, it was because of a very simple observation. Those things that affect people the most are political decisions and economic systems. Political decisions can mean the difference between legal discrimination, genocide, or progressive equality. Economic systems decide whether we can afford fairer policies, and how our society is organised to achieve things. These two aspects of society rule how we live, how we work, and all the important things about our lives. Yet there is currently no rational or agreeable way to theorise political or economic systems, because morality – the principles which underpin our political and economic goals – are considered to be *subjective*. So even if we were to have the most advanced political and economic forecasting systems you could imagine, we still couldn't benefit from significantly advanced evidenced-based politics and economics, because our principles are subjective and not based on evidence. Evidenced-based politics and economics will forever be a dream whilst we cannot agree what an evidence-based theory of ethics looks like.

Of course, there are counterarguments to this statement that I would be remiss not to mention. You could argue that we already have an implicit, broad agreement on morality (so it isn't subjective); after all, we do have laws, and new laws come into existence each year. Similarly, outdated judgements are often amended or removed.

I would argue that whilst this is partly true – this does represent how our laws work – it misses the point. Laws currently change when politicians or judges feel safe enough with society's opinion in order to make a new judgement. This isn't a rational moral code, with which one could build sensible systems upon, but rather a collection of things that happened to have been proposed because of their relation to our naturally evolving opinions.

As a result, certain things rarely improve and have never been solved: crime rates, homelessness, wealth inequality, third world poverty, global warming etc. To solve these kinds of issues you need smart, evidence-based systems of politics and economics which can evolve and develop based on new evidence. Ways of fairly attributing resources to solve big problems. Yet, at current, we have all the evidence we could possibly need to show that climate change is a man-made disaster waiting to happen, but political and economic opinions and intentions have stopped any significant action on it.

Climate change is indeed the best example of the problem with our current subjective morality. It isn't powerful interests that keep us from stopping climate change – though it might seem that way – but rather our inability to change a system which was never properly formed. We didn't just decide upon democracy because it was a good idea, it socially evolved. Similarly, we didn't just decide upon capitalism, it evolved. I happen to think that both of these systems are a good idea, but both require structural changes in order to best suit their purpose in serving citizens.

These structural changes don't currently happen, partly because there is no precedent for people sitting down and completely analysing and amending our entire ways of life. The reason there is no precedent for this comes full circle back to my opening remarks: our moral and personal values are viewed as just that – personal – so there is no firm ground that everyone can build an evidenced-based system from. So people have opinions about things that bear some or no relation to reality, and we end up compromising based on opinions, rather than acting based on facts. And no one thinks sitting down and theorising a better system is a worthwhile spend of time, because no one thinks it possible.

This is why I released *Rational Morality*, but also why I continue to work in the area – asking questions such as 'what does a rational code of ethics look like?' but also 'what would an objectively good economic system be?' and 'what political system is best at achieving this?'

These three are intertwined, with each intimately affecting the others, but the weightiest of them all is certainly morality. If we can solve the idea of what rational ethics looks like, and take it much further than simply what a mutually prosperous coordination looks like, then we have a base on which to move towards an evidenced political and economic system. We can move towards the most capable and effective versions that are possible, benefiting from the collective and ever growing knowledge of humankind. There's little doubt about that, in my mind. There's also little doubt that this goal is a good thing – the best kind of society we could possibly create, at any given time – and thus we need to start seriously discussing it.

IS YOUR BRAIN ENTIRELY RELIANT ON CONTEXT?

There seems to be an unwritten agreement in politics that certain jobs require extraordinary talents – talents that deserve to be recompensed at obscene rates. I am, of course, primarily referring to bankers. After the banking crash of the late 2000s, banker bonuses continued at high levels, with massive bonus payments even after the great failure. There was widespread acceptance that regardless of your opinion, we need to be able to attract 'top talent' to these jobs.

I'm not saying that isn't true to some degree. The most experienced managers, for instance, can often be the best at managing situations. However try to put it into context for a second, and it should become obvious that there should be an abundance of decent enough bankers around. After all, what does it require? A brief understanding of maths (most of it isn't doing sums in your head, so don't worry about that), a grasp of economic trends (which should be taught in most economics programs) and a grasp of the companies/countries previous trends, which should certainly be learned as expertise grows in this sector. Most moderately intelligent people, with an education in economics and some experience in the sector, should be able to do the job.

Likewise, the most senior would – all other things being equal – be better at it. After all, none of us can see the future so experience is one of the few relevant factors. If you want further proof, consider that those senior bankers who are meant to be the best at it, failed to predict their poor choices to the degree that a global recession was caused (as their knowledge was inadequate). If there was a test for how good bankers are, surely it would be whether they can do their job well enough to stop the banks playing a large part in a self-defeating global recession. They failed that test. This doesn't make them bad, it simply shows that they are employees, 100% human, and probably not anymore 'extraordinary' than potentially hundreds of people underneath them, had those hundreds had the same training.

The context of talking about complicated sounding economics makes us agree with the idea of extraordinary talent, whereas the added detail of what bankers job's actually involve is likely to make us more quizzical about it. Therefore, context can lead us to entirely different opinions on the same issue, even though we are the same person with the same level of knowledge.

But perhaps I'm trying to be too specific with my examples. Let's talk about everyday events instead. The sentence 'John bought a flannel to wash his face with' is an entirely valid one. Imagine the word flannel in that correct sentence, now say the below in your head.

Flannel. Flannel. Flannel. Flannel... Flannel.

Flannel. Flannel. Flannel.

Does it still seem right? Keep saying it in your head. Flannel. Flannel. Flannel.

In a reasonably short period of time, that word is going to start sounding bizarre to you. Like you've never before considered what an odd sound it consists of. Were it not written in front of you, by a published author trying to make a point, you might start to doubt that the word even exists. In fact, if you're really odd, there's a chance that you've done this before with words: repeated them to the degree that you wonder if it's actually pronounced like that, or whether it is even a real word.

Once you remove that veneer of context from the word – even if the context was there just 20 seconds ago – your brain can be quickly tricked into doubting things that it would otherwise be really confident of.

You could theoretically not hear the word 'flannel' for 20 years, yet then recognise it instantly next to a word you hear every minute of the day, without even noticing you've recognised it. You might not even register that you haven't heard it for 20 years. Yet you could become unsure that it even existed by simply taking it out of context for 20 seconds.

If you want further proof, we can go even simpler. If you have both of your legs, you probably walk without even thinking about it. Well, stand up and go for a two-minute walk, but just as you set off start thinking about what your legs and arms should do. Be prepared for an awkward two minutes, where you're suddenly going to experience every overthinker's favourite anxiety: "How could I have forgotten how to walk!"

If you can't walk for whatever reason – perhaps you don't have the use of your legs – it even works with breathing. You do it all the time without realising, your brain automatically manages... yet... as soon as you put it into a context of conscious control, you might just start worrying that if you stop thinking about it, you will stop breathing.

Our struggle to continue our normal, often unconscious activities, once we consciously analyse them, is interesting. But it is more telling that this unintentional struggle exists in our ability to reason (like with the example about the bankers): if we are presented with something in a more detailed or conscious context, it can completely change our opinion to what we initially thought. In some ways, this sums up our brains: smart, developed, yet like a piece of software that doesn't work quite right once elements are moved out of place/order.

It should also shed some light on how we make decisions: context is important, and we should reserve judgement on things that we don't have much information about.

OBSESSION WITH CULTURE OVER HUMANKIND

"I DON'T **CARE** IF THE DOG IS **ATTACKING** THE MAIL MAN.
IF HE'S **NOT** WEARING A **TARTAN SKIRT**, I'M NOT **HELPING**."

Scotland is a country which is proud of its past and traditions. In this sense, it's atypical of almost every other country in the world. People here are very keen to have their national identity retained; maintaining and celebrating traditions and cultural resonances is how they do it.

A great example of this would be the country's love of the traditional language of Gaelic. Around 1% of Scotland's population can speak Gaelic, yet it retains a status as a celebrated language. The BBC upholds a Gaelic speaking TV channel, road signs around the country are translated into it, and even organisations like the Scottish NHS translate the footers in their emails from English to Gaelic.

There's no great pragmatic need for this, of course. Around the same number of people in Scotland can speak Polish as Gaelic, and probably many more of the Polish speakers would have trouble with English, whereas most Gaelic speakers would be fluent in English. But keeping Gaelic on a pedestal allows Scotland some sort of link to its past. Though, we must forget that Gaelic was never even spoken through all of Scotland... but let's ignore that for a second, and indulge the idea that it is "Scotland's culture".

Very few people ever question why such a cultural celebration is necessary.

The desire to have links with a past – whether real or imagined – creates large barriers to any multi-cultural society. After all, our desperate desire to maintain history in the present, rather than allow it to be confined in books or art, surely has more of an effect in society than we like to think.

Primarily, the problem with glorifying the past is in nationalism. Things like Gaelic, or odd toasts during Ceilidhs (Scottish cultural dances), or even celebrating an old-fashioned and probably womanising poets day, seem like reasonably mild and inoffensive items on their own. And they might be. Similarly, these things also have positives: they push a real sense of belonging and identity among the people who take joy from them. Belonging with other people in the 'in-group', who also share the same attachments/physical characteristics of a Scotsman. But we shouldn't forget the negatives.

Because every country is desperate to have its own culture – with which to induct every citizen who is raised there – it often really repels people from other cultures, creating a divide. It means that migrants tend to create communities of their own, within new countries, and it causes friction with those who view them as outsiders. Indeed, the fear that many Scottish people have of Muslims wanting to enact Islamic law, is arguably not so much based on an understanding of the problems of religion, or prejudice, but rather a fear of another culture, or another culture's religion, taking over here. Whereas in fact Christianity – "our own religion" – is the same nonsense: Christians denouncing homosexuals are no better than Muslims denouncing homosexuals.

Indeed, a rational society wouldn't be overly bothered about becoming a different culture *per se*, as our current culture should be something we can marvel at and enjoy without having attachment in that manner. A rational culture should want to protect its education system, evolving moral rules, perhaps even its defence system, but it should also want to culturally evolve as well. If Islamic culture would make our own more interesting and useful, we should embrace it. And if we disagree with it, we should do so on rational grounds – arguing against its treatment of women or homosexuals – not due to it simply being a different culture.

But we don't, and Scotland is a great piece of evidence in showing that we don't. Two distinct groups – Gaelic speakers and Polish speakers – are roughly equal in number there. Yet Gaelic is celebrated and reinforced. Indeed, such a small number speak it, that one really has to go out of one's way to learn it; reinforcement in certain areas is all that has maintained Gaelic. Whilst Polish is often a first language, but people who speak that language are ignored, often vilified. Tradition has well and truly won out against rational analysis.

I'm unsure that any article under 1,000 words can do justice to the great battle which our societies host between culture and social evolution. But I'm not sure I've ever heard it discussed in the media, which leads me to ask whether or not we're even aware of it?

As an ethicist, I'm very aware that deep attachments and unwillingness to change cultures are the strongest enemy of social justice. For many years the American south held that owning slaves was a cultural belief – a civil war was fought to defend it. The ramifications of which are felt to this day. Celebrating and cementing cultural phenomena is something which should be done with rational caution.

SHOULD THE OLYMPICS BE MODERNISED?

I'm very rarely proud of my nationality. That's not because I consider being British to be a negative label, but rather because I rarely see anything impressive about having the good fortune to have been born in a certain location.

Indeed, I can only recall two times I felt truly proud to be a Brit. One was at the opening ceremony of the Olympics held here in 2012. Director Danny Boyle created a beautiful, mesmerising show that championed all that is good about Britain. From the NHS, to our great engineers, to even having an alternative, folk-punk musician (who relatively few but me would have heard of prior to that moment) opening the whole thing. In that moment I felt like I belonged to a country which had achieved things, and had led the world in looking after its people, and proudly stood up to be different. We also symbolised the union of four great nations, sitting independently as one. A great progress from our days of aggressive empire building.

The second time, rather more shallowly, was in 2016 at the next Olympics. Team GB won medal after medal, breaking its record from London, finishing second in the medal table behind only the USA. Indeed, we won gold in more separate sports than the US, which really made me feel proud. These athletes might occasionally have been funded by sponsorship money, but they were initially sponsored by government funding, and public funding in the guise of national lottery grants.

Which makes the argument I am about to make sound altogether a little self-defeating. I believe the Olympics badly needs modernising, and part of that should involve dissolving a lot of the disciplines and events in which Britain is actually very successful.

I think the Olympics, at least here in the UK, has become even more important than it ever was. I remember staying up to see our British rowers win gold in Sydney in 2000, as it seemed important and rare. Now, with more countries winning medals than ever before, and with more sports than ever before, the entire thing seems to be a worldwide event like no other.

CRITICAL THINKING ARTICLES

Yet if these are to be the true pinnacles of sport, we must indeed make them match that statement. I won't go into a listing exercise of all the sports I think are unsuitable, but I will make some arguments about a few.

The 100m is the pinnacle of the track events at the Olympics, as well as one of the most exciting. Similarly, it makes some sense to also have a 200m, 400m, 800m etc. What would not make sense is having a 100m>65kg, 100m>85kg etc. Undoubtedly that would suit some athletes who cannot compete with the strength and height that Usain Bolt has, but it would pointlessly separate the field so as 'fastest man in the world' no longer meant anything. Whilst I see the point in separating female and male sportspeople (in disciplines where it is necessary – in fencing, for instance, it shouldn't be), I see no point in separating weights or heights.

Primarily this is done in sports like taekwondo or wrestling to make use of the facilities – ensuring the hosts don't have one location hosting only a few tens of events. But you can have juniors competing, or world championships held in other disciplines at the same time, whilst still keeping the Olympic events separate from the rest. If someone is better because they are heavier, there is no more need to give a separate competition to the lighter than there is a separate 100m to the slower. My weight means I will naturally be worse at some sports, and I should accept that. I can still partake in them, I am just naturally worse at them. There's no shame in that.

Which brings us nicely to those sports that create divisions to reward those with skills at slower or less effective techniques: here's looking at you, swimming. In 2016, for instance, the USA won 16 gold medals in swimming (33 medals in it overall). These included swimming like a 'butterfly' over different distances, and swimming like a 'butterfly' in a team over different distances, swimming backward over different distances, and swimming backwards in a team over different distances, swimming without your torso rotating (breaststroke) over different distances, and doing so within a team over different distances. And, of course, doing all of these things in a medley, over different distances, on your own or in a team. If aliens were to judge our Olympics – our swimming events against our track and field events – they would wonder why we are so desperate to reward swimmers' artistic versions of their form, yet punish our land-dwelling brethren so badly. Swimming champion Michael Phelps won as many medals in 2016 alone, his final Olympics, as Jamaican athlete Usain Bolt – the greatest sprinter and fastest athlete who ever existed – could manage in his entire career.

We don't allow running backwards, running in silly shapes, or running in strict body movements as separate events, so neither should we allow swimming in those ways. Feel free to have swimming world championships in all these things, but let's not sully the Olympics with them. The Olympics should be for the great athletes – of which Phelps is one – fighting it out by moving through the water as fast as possible. The only 'stroke' event should be freestyle, and the fastest individuals or teams over each distance should be rewarded. Not only would it mean more to the athletes – as athletes could not accumulate gazillions of gold medals for simply being good at one thing – it would also be more palatable and easy to understand for us spectators. This is meant to be the greatest show on Earth, the best athletes in the world competing. You don't see Jamaica sending a sprint-backwards team to the track, it would be ridiculous.

There are also some sports which are simply bad fits. One category of this are sports in which someone other than the sportsperson is really winning the race. Here we're looking at you, horse-sports. Show-jumping, for example, hardly seems a test of ability for the human so much as the horse. Indeed, bringing horses into these massive arenas full of cheering humans hardly seems the most humane event, either, no matter how much love these riders profess for their horses. But, either way, a horse that is good at jumping fences – and better than other horses at it – will always do better than horses that aren't, so long as the 'rider' pulls the reigns at the right time. That's barely even a sport at all. It's the same test of skill as Bop-It, which you will notice is not an Olympic event.

Unfortunately, the rest of the equestrian events fare little better. Dressage is, essentially, riding in fancy clothes on a horse while it does silly walks around a square (which she no doubt has been tortured to repeat until she gets it right – among god knows what other cruel training practices). The judges then decide how well the horse did the silly walks, and award it points. It is the most absurd sport I've ever watched. And 'eventing' is a mixture of these horse events, to test the horse and reward the rider. The whole event really is past its sell by date. By the way, if you think my bias against our competitors in the US leads to my dislike of swimming, it should be pointed out that Team GB are very good on horses.

Talk of judges within the silly horse walk event leads to the last events I will go after by name, the events where judges decide who 'won'. In Rio 2016, there was enormous controversy about this, and even judges sent home from the boxing bouts, as they weren't managing to agree with other judges about who won. If things are so artistic in any event, so much so that the result has to regularly be decided by judges, then how much of a sport really is it? If it's subjective, it's an art, or a game, not a sport.

Sports like taekwondo and fencing may get around this – my dictatorial attitudes on culling Olympic sports are open to argument about these – due to them using actual sensors to decide who gained points by virtue of who actually scored points. Like football, rugby, basketball or most other big sports, these seem to make sense. But boxing (in most cases knock outs do not decide the winner, judges do) certainly shouldn't escape the cull. And neither should bizarre 'sports' like diving – a 'sport' where all competitors seem able to do the same manoeuvres, but the winners are those creating the least splash when entering the pool... I kid you not. And gymnastics? A beautiful art form, sure, but it's entirely subjective and not a sport in any way. One spectator's most cherished move to watch may not even be good enough for a last place finish, and the most agile or strongest are often not rewarded at all; often times they are relegated in favour of the person who landed in the most steady manner.

I should also quickly mention that cycling – a sport that Team GB currently rocks at every Olympics – should also be cut back. Or, at the very least, events like the individual sprint should actually be about going fastest around the track, and not, as currently happens, be decided by two cyclists slowly tailing and watching each other – sometimes stopping completely together – before doing a final tactical dash against the other one during the last lap. The winner being the one who did it before the other could notice fast enough to catch up. That's a playground game called 'tag', not a sport.

Of course, the Olympics has a great deal of sports left when you take these sports – and often just the offending events of each sport – away. But it also needs more actual, globally popular sports adding. I'm not a fan of golf at all, but it's inclusion in Rio 2016 was a no-brainer. It is a smart and popular sport, and it should be included. Just as tennis was a few years ago too. Baseball/softball will be with us in Tokyo, another 'finally' moment for what is an obvious choice. But what about sports like cricket – one that nations (such as Sri Lanka and Pakistan) who do not traditionally do well at the Olympics would have a shot at? What about turning rugby sevens into rugby union – even if it means only having the quarterfinals onwards, for sake of allowing the athletes recovery? What about American football? What about squash? The list must be endless. And it should be long, after all, as this is about the best of each sport: we need to do away with endless types of swimming and horse riding etc, and introduce various actual sports.

Moreover, what about making the soccer element more serious? Currently soccer is allowed, but only as an under 23's tournament. That's bizarre. Major tennis and golf stars have shown that the Olympics mean something to professional athletes who have lucrative careers elsewhere. Just ask the Williams sisters, or Justin Rose. Olympic football must either evolve to be a full international tournament, else a five a side indoor game, or something else which is the pinnacle of its type. Not a junior competition.

I'll finish my argument by noting that the current Olympic roster includes the triathlon – a gruelling swimming, cycling and running event (one after the other). It includes the heptathlon – a mixture of running, jumping and throwing sports, crowning true athletic prowess across disciplines. But it also includes the 'modern' pentathlon, which consists of swimming, running, PISTOL FIRING, FENCING and SHOW JUMPING. And in the pistol firing during the modern pentathlon, there is a slight delay between the trigger being pulled and the laser actually appearing on the target, in order to simulate the shooting of a MUSKET. It is still named 'modern' despite first appearing in 1912, and looking like an LSD-induced trip into a gameshow-meets-spaghetti western.

The Olympics needs modernising, I rest my case.

WHAT ARE THE RULES OF SATIRE?

Following the terrorist attack on the offices of French satirist magazine Charlie Hebdo in January 2015, the world saw an unrelated refugee crisis as Syrians fled to Europe. One of the enduring, tragic and most printed images in world media was of a drowned Syrian refugee boy who was called Aylan. It seemed to sum up the grief of a despairing planet, which was suffering trauma after trauma.

The news on the first day of 2016 centred on New Year celebrations in Cologne, Germany, which had seen a mass sexual assault on women by a seemingly organised group of men. It was reported that many of the men were immigrants, and the predictable fearmongering about immigration was then invoked by various right-wing sources. Some of it was based on truth – some refugees do have religious, often intolerant views of women – whilst much more swept into hysteria.

On the anniversary of the Hebdo shootings, a few days later, a resilient Charlie Hebdo publication did what it is famous for. It shocked the word with the most biting satire. A picture of the tragic death of Aylan, and the suggestion (made as comically as it could) that in losing Aylan we have lost an 'ass groper in Germany'.

Defenders of Hebdo say the cartoon is simply lampooning our bizarre, hypocritical views; we pick out tragedies in order to decry the plight of Syrian refugees and then jump on the minority of criminals among them to fearmonger. Critics, understandably, say it goes too far. After all, the image of a dead toddler washed up on a beach is not something to make light of, nor use for financial gain. That toddler likely still has some family, some friends, and they should never have to see such a cartoon regardless of the intellectual purity or humour of the idea behind it. Whether it be satire or not, find another way to make your point.

This isn't the first time satire has come under the microscope – not even recently. The Golden Globes are regularly hosted by Ricky Gervais, who is famous for using it as a stage for just the kind of satire that makes you cringe. Gervais plays the character of a straight-talking idiot, in essence, who will crack jokes about anything. Usually aiming directly at the big stars in the crowd, and taking it a step further than other comedians do.

In early 2016 he hosted them again, and drew laughs for his com-ments on the campaign for equal pay for female actresses. As a person, he obviously endorses the move, yet his joke told the viewers that minimum wage workers up and down the land had been shocked that Jennifer Lawrence was being asked to survive on only $25 million a year, and were keen to protest for her. This satire, ironically, was nothing to do with the sexist pay gap in Hollywood (and wider society) and instead referenced the pay gap between screen-stars (like himself) and normal working people.

Like with the Hebdo cartoon, the worry is that the audience is using the satire to ingrain its racist or sexist views, rather than spotting the irony or lampoon as it is intended. Yet, the likes of comedians such as Stewart Lee use satire regularly, whilst rarely being accused of the same thing. Some of his shows deconstruct the irony onstage – allowing him to explicitly and humorously point out that he doesn't want people laugh-ing at it for the wrong reasons, and asking those kinds of people to leave etc – but what of the rest?

One of Lee's routines, from his well-known 'Carpet Remnants World' tour, sees him speaking the words of Americans who have funny and offensive opinions about what they would like to see happen to Osama Bin Laden. They range from gross sexually demeaning suggestions, to odd religiously insensitive comments about Muslims. Why is Lee not accused of sexism or religious intolerance, on the same lines that Gervais and Hebdo are?

The answer is in the definable yet strangely ambiguous rules of satire. Lee sets up the American's quotes with them firmly in the firing line, rather than the terrorist they are speaking about, and he ends it by pointing out they weren't real quotes, and comically blaming the audience for discriminatingly believing they definitely were. For most, the fact he made these offensive words up himself, to get laughs, would make his situation worse. Yet the way he builds the joke is carefully done in a way that dictates laughter at the satire/irony: something that is neither easy nor always possible to do. Similarly, Lee knows his audience, and even spends large parts of his show lampooning the parts of the audience who might not have seen him before, or might not get 'deeper' jokes that he tells.

Lee both intellectually absolves himself, but also places guilt onto the audience throughout. Similarly, his demeanour in the routine is as if he is presenting or lecturing rather than looking for jokes. He regularly polls as one of the comedian's favourite comedians, and his expertise at building routines to be funny, smart and not to misuse satire, is one of the reasons for that. Indeed, Gervais was a fan of Lee prior to releasing his own stand-up.

The strange thing about my analysis of why Lee gets away with his satire, is that it isn't as rationally sound as I would like. It kind of makes sense, but the rules of satire are so subjective, and so dependent on the way it is presented, or structured, that it almost defies a good, structural analysis. Were I to recreate the same routine as Lee, but not get the right emphasis, the right tone etc, I might be presenting something that doesn't obey the 'rules' of satire in the same way.

If we are to learn anything about these ambiguous rules, though, it is that there is a difference between things which do successfully make ironic reference, and those which are obviously open to miscomprehension. Hebdo's cartoon simply sits there, with no explanation, for the world's media to see, at a time when the world's media was watching. Gervais' routine was not to his normal fans, but to the worlds media again, with the occasional laugh, but with ample opportunity to be misrepresented. Lampooning our hypocrisy about refugees and Hollywood are both potentially ideal forms of satire, yet unlike with Lee's routine, there is no smart casing to protect the sentiments in either.

Finding that casing, of course, is harder than it sounds. There are a variety of banal, dull and wannabe edgy comedians who offend people for money, and there are equal numbers of them who over-explain to the point that it feels like a lecture or textbook rather than satire. That's what makes these ambiguous rules so difficult to learn, and arguably impossible to define. The kinds of things that experienced, quality stand-up comedians can do, by virtue of refining a piece for months on end. This is something that is not so easy to do with weekly publications, or when rehearsing for awards shows.

Arguably, the only easy rule is that if you think you're being paid to offend people, and your only defence is, "It's satire, I'm joking!" then you're not balancing it right. Yes, many people with your opinions, who know something about you, will probably understand your intentions. But, no, calling it satire and stating your intentions were pure shouldn't clear your conscience about taking the gig.

Comedians and satirists are like any other form of media, in being a way of transferring norms to other members of the public. For people like Gervais, and the liberal voices of Charlie Hebdo, the craft should be a complex one of transferring your rationale effectively and humorously, not simply of spurting out material followed by defensive claims like you are making 'art' or 'a statement about defending free speech' or, worse, 'it's only a joke'. The former is smart, constructed, thoughtful art. The latter is pretention.

WHY IS THE ABSURD FUNNY?

The British TV show *Shooting Stars*, endured a cult-like following in the UK. It pulled in large viewing figures, and went on for several series. It centred as a quiz panel show format, but with real questions mixed with completely made up ones, some that didn't even make sense. The guy tasked with keeping the scores – the now famous comedy actor Matt Lucas – always sat at a drum kit, for little apparent reason other than to drum randomly, and dressed as a baby. He was replaced in the final seasons by a different actor, who played the character Angelos, dressed in a long brown coat, carrying a bag of shopping around, and making strange techno noises on a keyboard.

One of the enduring and most repeated moments on the show is when the characters and guests beckon down a cheap cardboard cut out (normally of a dove) with categories on it. All the while, the entire show was regularly interrupted by bizarre comments, sketches and inaudible songs, yet constantly treated as if it were any other quiz show.

The most memorable thing for me was a simple sketch where Matt Lucas – dressed as a gym teacher, rather than a baby this time – stood in the middle of the stage with simple, playful music accompanying him. He put on a deep voice and sternly, randomly repeated the word 'peanuts' in a tone one might expect of a commanding officer in the army.

Lucas did not get far through the short performance before he, the audience, the other actors and the guests were all in fits of laughter. His last few 'peanuts' were either missed completely due to hysterical laughing, else giggled out. All that had happened, may I remind you, is the word 'peanuts' was being spoken by someone dressed as a gym teacher, whilst music played.

That scene is funny to so many people only because it's utterly absurd: Matt Lucas appears dressed as a gym teacher for no good reason; the sketch has no real relevance to what happened before, and is not necessary for what happens afterwards in the show; and it doesn't actually make any sense. Why would a gym teacher be sternly shouting 'peanuts' with his hands behind his back?

Those that are more keenly attuned to comedic theory will have noticed that it doesn't just take advantage of the old comedy rule regarding the absurd, but it also uses repetition to great effect: once you've done something absurd and mildly funny, quite often it actually gets funnier, because you know how funny it was the first time. It is more absurd to do it twice than once. And, sometimes, when the humour of it dies down, enough repetition can even bring it back: after all, what's more absurd than carrying on with something utterly absurd, which is meant to be funny, even after it is has stopped being funny?

Why do we find the absurd funny, though? We can trace most behavioural patterns back to evolutionary heritage fairly easily: everything from apathy and kindness, to anger and hatred. We can even find good reasons why we seem to see patterns in randomness: because we lose nothing for spotting patterns of danger when there is none, but we lose a lot if we fail to spot patterns of danger. Yet why do we have a humorous sense for the absurd, the unexpected, or the oddly repetitive? What evolutionary role has it played that means it exists now, or, perhaps, what evolutionary trait is it a by-product of?

This is not an easy question. One might start by trying to tie it to socially important traits: after all, the presence of someone else laughing seems to be catalyst for laughter itself. I don't mean a simple laughing noise, but rather the sight of someone in tears of laughter makes our mouths curve upwards, almost in empathetic humour. A by-product of those mirror neurons that have us feeling sensations when we see them in others. Perhaps, then, laughter is like other social habits; a way of cementing social bonds – perhaps sharing an opinion on an event might be useful for bringing us together?

This might make some sense. People who are better at forging social bonds are likely to be better at reproducing. Especially in a world before schools, bars and dating websites made it easier to learn social norms and communicate with strangers. So this might explain why humour plays such a large role in human life. But it doesn't explain why it exists in the first place: at what point did someone look at another human scratching her ear like a wolf, and then laugh? Why does humour even exist?

Perhaps we need to look at the other side of social bonds, the negative reinforcement side. As much as humour may have, at some point, played a cementing bond between people, perhaps it was initially a form of ridicule. And in turn, was ridicule itself an aggressive, non-violent form of hierarchical cement?

For example, an alpha male may have used ridicule as a tool to put someone in their place without having to expand the energy of resorting to violence. Here we start to happen upon why it might exist. Our social tendencies, and rapid social evolution, did a great deal to develop many of our traits: whether it be the important ideas of altruism or kindness, or scheming and playing social games. There is no reason that ridicule could not have evolved into society through this method too: a form of passive aggression, which allowed alphas and leaders to keep their reputation and standing in place.

Historically, looking at the role of humour would perhaps help to support this idea. When we think back to humour in medieval times, we do conjure up images of jesters or jokers entertaining the monarchs. Powerful people ridiculing these entertainers for their own entertainment, reinforcing their own status among the rest of the audience. So the idea is a plausible one.

From ridicule, humour comes reasonably rationally and easily. After all, people have happened upon what it means to share laughter or humour, so for this to be quickly socially evolved into other types of humour is understandable. People would naturally enjoy ridicule of other people, as it cements someone else as the target rather than them, while they may often even get to be the aggressor.

It does feel a little uncomfortable to be drawing the spectrum of humour back solely to ridicule, though it makes sense to do so. From dark seeds can come flowering bushes.

So why do we find the absurd funny? Quite possibly because it innately manipulates our will to ridicule someone, as harsh as that sounds. People of all backgrounds can watch Matt Lucas stating 'peanuts' at a camera and laugh. If my experience is anything to go by, groups of people in an office can fall about for entire afternoons doing just that, on that one scene. We may even think he is some kind of raw comedy genius, yet deep down it is our instinct to take part in ridicule that is being raised. Fancy that.

And if you think about it all comedy, all humour, comes back to that. Why did I think it was funny to write 'fancy that' at the end of the last sentence, for instance? Well, I'm trying to impress you by being a jester, by putting unexpectedly out of place terms in my paragraphs that might make you laugh or at least read my words in a more positive and light hearted way. This unexpected word placement is absurd and non-conformist, and earlier in human history would have been ridiculed, not simply laughed at.

Why, then, do I have the desire to do it, if it is the path to – and only to – ridicule? Presumably because ridicule is better than being brutally beaten, and deep down that is a safety mechanism I have evolved? Or, more likely, humour has simply changed uses within society: we now have laughter and humour that is completely free from ridicule. Smart comedians arouse our admiration rather than ridicule, and now they can even warrant sexual attractiveness and/or long-term mate status etc.

WHY DO WE EMBRACE LABELS, BUT NOT EVIDENCE?

Liberals, conservatives, centrists, leftists, libertarians, socialists, anarchists, greens, Marxists, nationalists, democrats and republicans. Our modern political environment is obsessed with tribalism and labels, like at no other time in history.

Yet, in societies which have benefited so greatly from enlightenment thinking and the scientific revolution, we seem almost opposed to the only label that really matters: rationalism.

Rationalism doesn't have perspectives; it is, as defined by the *Oxford Dictionary*, "the practice or principle of basing opinions and actions on reason and knowledge rather than on religious belief or emotional response". Yet every major political party and social movement in the world ignores it.

Instead our political systems resemble a 20-seater car, with 20 steering wheels. Each perspective – created by the basic emotion or intuitions of its leaders and members – picking and choosing the evidence and statistics that best fits its goals. And in result, our institutions veer left, right, or around in circles, almost randomly depending on events that are affecting the powerful opinions (in government or media) in that very moment.

The reason for this is as obvious as is it is mistaken. Whilst physics, chemistry, biology, maths, sociology, psychology and every other area of academic study has steered towards evidence-based results, people believe politics is based on morality. And morality, we believe, is a personal, spiritual, else subjective choice. There are no universal facts in morality – no evidence which can tell us what is right or wrong – so we must pick a perspective and stick with it.

Yet, myself and many others have written extensively on the problems with assuming morality is subjective. So long as we all want to live in society, and co-habit with one another, we have a shared base from which we'll want to create a moral code. And as long as we can agree on basic moral principles – such as, for instance, that harm to others should be avoided wherever possible (defining what 'harm' entails), or people should be respected wherever possible (defining what respect entails) –

then we've gotten basic moral rules which we should extend rationally, based on evidence and logic.

We do half of this, in that we do have certain shared moral beliefs (barely anyone believes murderers should be free to murder again, for example, which means we're agreeing about something) and also that political movements almost always try to persuade people to their point of view based on moral reasons. The problem with the former is that we get there in the longest, most winding road possible, by having perspective led political parties propose or oppose each moral change. A shorter way would be in discussing the evidence/reason, and allowing logic to lead the way (not arguing a perspective once it has been defeated in a logical manner). The latter (political movements using moral appeals) is problematic as they tend to both ignore a balanced view of evidence, and also ignore when more basic and agreed moral rules disagree with them.

This isn't, of course, to say that voting for political representation is a pointless endeavour. For example, to garner progress in the modern world, our systems have become so muddled and ineffective that all parties consider it necessary to abuse reason and evidence in order to achieve their goals. Abusing the means to achieve the ends is necessary because everyone else does it.

When conservatives or republicans stand for election, for example, it would almost always make sense to vote against them. The opponents of those parties (the left) are almost equally ignorant of evidence and reason, yet the means of agenda setting for the political right is through the interests of the rich, minority of citizens. It is thus almost always better and more democratic to vote for the interests of an agenda which are not set in this manner.

Serious arguments must be made against both sides, though. If one truly believes that their opinion is correct, then arguing based on evidence and reason is the way to prove it. Currently politicians work through soundbites, persuasive topical opinions, and veering public opinion in their own direction by shouting louder than their opponents. But all politicians still have to debate one another, at one time or another. Pre-election leaders' debates occur in most countries now, and in those debates a strong stance for reason and evidence – put forth by leaders who are skilled at spotting the illogic and exposing it – cannot fail to have an effect. However, if we keep voting for leaders who look good, or create good soundbites, we won't be putting people with these abilities into the position to significantly change things.

More than anything, a change on behalf of evidence comes from a necessary change in the political system. In fact, we don't even need a complete overhaul, simple tweaks would work. Why not employ neutral, talented academics – with an affinity for reason and a team with which to research evidence – to feedback and provide actual answers to give to the public, on weekly debates in parliament? Why not make sure that the speaker in the House of Commons – the person responsible for making sure debate flows productively – is someone who is capable of using reason, and capable of spotting when someone is not answering a question?

In a court of law, we ensure that judges are able to spot when defendants aren't providing sufficient answers to back up their claims, yet in parliament we allow politicians to say absolutely anything they like, when they should be defending their policies with reason. And as long as their opponent only has a certain number of chances to speak (say six), then the ruling party can evade answers/rational analysis. It should be the speaker – or some sort of moderator – that provides the check of democracy, the check that the government is acting in the way they claim, or in consistency with their stated policies. And more than anything, if the prime minister cannot answer questions posed, we shouldn't limit prime minister questions to 30 or 60 minutes, allowing him a set time to bluff, we should force answers, for as long as needed, else action should be taken against him.

These people are running the country, and we currently do not have a sufficient system for holding them to account to reason and evidence. Were technology to be limited in relation to reason in the same way – were evidence-based companies able to be shouted out, and opportunities for evidence progression limited – I would likely have no computer to write these articles on, and there would probably be no way to print on mass so could you read it. Kindles and e-readers would be a fanciful idea, printed books themselves may be even be a thing of dreams. We've relied on evidence-based reasoning so long when it comes to technology that we take it for granted, forgetting what life would look like without industries that embraced the methodology of testing ideas and figuring out what does and doesn't work.

Yet in politics, things have barely moved on in hundreds of years. We now pay lip service to equality and progress, but things move so slowly – and often in the wrong direction – precisely because we haven't made an effort to improve the method itself. We celebrate the goals we achieve which seem to be in line with reason, like universal suffrage or animal welfare, but we don't ever bother improving the system. Therein lies the problem with politics. Left or right, liberal or conservative, democrat or anarchist: you should all be dumping your labels and perspectives, and aiming at rationalism. We now know that morality is consensual and rational in its ever-increasing extensions, so we don't need to work with political 'perspectives' from posh kids who are educated to be good at arguing.

WASTE AND THE BACK OF A SOFA ANALOGY

Most of us will recognise that no system is perfect. Combustion engines in cars don't just create the energy to power the car, they give off heat energy and produce exhaust fumes which a perfectly designed engine would be able to neutralise, and use to power the movement instead. Voting cards on election days are made to be as simple and effective as possible, but there will always be someone who marks the wrong box, or reacts in the wrong way, unintentionally wasting their vote. Even the best made and most expensive TVs heat up, failing to turn all of the electricity it uses into picture quality, whilst many speaker systems fail to cope with the full and infinitely varied spectrum of sound that could come their way, and most can experience vibrations or 'tinny' effects when rare sounds are transmitted.

The point I'm getting at is that no system works perfectly. However beautiful or perfect the maths and physics involved, most systems, in reality, cannot be made to a perfect standard. But we get over it. It can be summed up by the sofa analogy: our sofas have holes down the back, and we could lose pound coins down there, but it's better than not having a sofa. A reasonable amount of waste is accepted and expected. Of course you could actually just buy a sofa without the hole down the back, and it could still arguably be as comfy… but hey, I'm proving my point: even analogies can't be perfect!

The types of system that seem least likely to be perfect are those involving people; people are machines functioning at incredibly complex levels. They each consist of billions of cells and are capable of abstract and irrelevant thoughts, so compared to designing systems containing electricity, metal or plastic, human systems are unimaginably more complex. We are, after all, not just compositions of genetics, but we learn and develop based on our experiences. As a result, no two of us are anywhere near the same, and we can sometimes react to the same stimuli in bizarrely different ways. One person would kill so as not to be tied and tortured, whilst another might consider it a kinky thrill. We are a complicated and varied species, and those designing systems to organise our healthcare, or to run our economy, have a monumental task ahead of them.

That our societies function at all is remarkable, and probably reflective of our intelligence: in general, we realise that despite our differences we must cohabit on Earth. Still, what we have collectively organised in our individual groups is more remarkable. In the UK, for instance, we manage to utilise an advanced form of medical science, funded collectively and improving yearly, to look after one another. We employ people with passions for medicine and caring to do those jobs, so as we can live our lives enjoyably yet still endeavour to care for the weakest, oldest, youngest and the most ill. The system isn't perfect, but that word – remarkable – is appropriate when you consider how far we relatively hairless apes have come.

Yet, despite our progress, we seem to be taking for granted what we have created, and instead focusing on the weaknesses of systems in order to demonise people. We blame the NHS – not its politically motivated lack of funding – when people suffer through lack of care. No system can be perfect, especially not those which suffer through being understaffed and relying on the good nature of the most empathetic and caring people in society, rather than costing us all equally. We might pay chunks of our taxes to keep it running, but the extra unpaid hours that doctors, nurses and volunteers put in to keep the system functioning, and to keep people from suffering, means we aren't all paying our fair share.

Part of the excuse put forward from Conservative politicians – who are motivated classically by lessening the taxes of the wealthier – is that the NHS is wasteful and so taxes must be cut. Yet, we are asking the wrong questions on public services if we're more interested in the waste of any system than the output. We can always do things better, but using that as an excuse to limit the input of resources is not doing things better, it's just doing things cheaper. You don't make cars run more efficiently by putting less fuel in; you have to redesign the entire system if you're aiming at efficiency. And when Conservative politicians argued they were getting rid of 'bureaucrats' in the NHS, they removed huge swathes of people who were useful for organising care and connecting different sectors.

Those elderly patients who are suffering in the system don't just require doctors, nurses and carers – who already work long and often unpaid hours just to provide an average service due to understaffing. They also need people to intervene and monitor their care, uphold standards, arrange multi-disciplinary meetings between them, and keep the patient in mind. They need people to balance the books in GP practices and care homes; people to keep the supplies ordered in hospitals; and people to clean the floors and empty the bins. By removing those kinds of people you don't only make things more dangerous and worse for patients – as you end up spending expensive clinician time on what should be cheaper admin tasks – but you also increase the risk of patients being regularly admitted to hospital, which is the really expensive part of the system.

Of course some of those people are actually bureaucrats – but that is up to managers to deal with and organise, to get the best from people. If they fail, and some bureaucrats continue to exist in the system, we should consider it the same wastage as a warm combustion engine. Large and complicated systems will always involve waste of some sort. If we can't get rid of it in relatively simple mechanics, we certainly can't expect to do so in massive organisations focused on human health care. Better to deal with the waste as best we can, than cut it all out, cutting out half the engine or limiting the fuel in the process.

Yet, arguably, health care is not the biggest instance of 'back of the sofa' thinking. I think the welfare state is.

Every week, seemingly without fail, a mainstream TV channel, or a national newspaper, decides it will show us someone who is 'benefiting' a little too much from not working but instead being on benefits. It will show us stories of people with 20 children who earn tens of thousands of pounds a year by being on benefits, or it will show us stories of drug addicts who buy drugs with their benefits. The media's intention is to create an audience from which to profit – selling outrage to any scandal they can find – but its effect is in creating a distrust of the system by focusing on the waste rather than putting it in context.

Let's start at the beginning. Welfare is a necessary cost to the taxpayer, by any standard of human decency and fairness. Capitalism and modern economics can't exist without unemployment of some level (you need unemployed people, as they help create growth when they become employed), so someone will always be suffering that indignity. It is entirely unreasonable and irrational to decide we are going to have a capitalist system, then not compensate those that suffer because of it. Capitalism is the best form of economic system available to us, but we're structuring it wrong if we allow people to demonise/harm the necessary victims. As a result, we do provide 'benefits' to people who do not have a steady or sufficient income, and the vast majority of those compensated are exactly who are meant to be benefiting.

However – as with any system – some people will be able to claim benefits in an unfair manner. This is a very small percentage of total benefits paid out, but some people will work illegitimately whilst claiming benefits, whilst others won't want to work at all. All of which will seem unfair to people who do slave away in day jobs and pay for these benefits from their own wages. Further down the line, some people will have huge numbers of children, and be looked after by the state – which will seem parasitic to your average person who is in a hard-working job – and others will spend benefits on drugs instead of food, which to those same workers will seem to not be the point of benefits.

But, as I mentioned before, whereas these numbers of people might be vocal, louder, and scrutinised far more regularly on TV – a normal jobseeker is boring compared to a family of 15 living in squalor, or a drug addict living in a squat – they are a tiny majority.

However, let's assume them to be wasting taxpayers' money. That makes them the relative waste in the system. You can't feasibly uphold an unemployed person's dignity by giving them food vouchers for certain shops instead of money, just to spite the drug addict. And you can't force children into poverty by lessening the benefits of people with children, just to stop people having large amounts of children whilst on benefits.

To build a system which does care about people, foster a sense of belonging and an enthusiasm for hard work, and which works to eradicate child poverty, you need a system of benefits. And no system is perfect, no matter how good the intention, so we should expect there to be waste within that system.

If you want to teach people interesting things about the system, teach them how the alternatives to capitalism are more unfair, but how capitalism requires a certain level of unemployment to function. That would help to change the perception of the unemployed, especially those chronically unemployed. Without them there is no capitalism, which needs a pool of the unemployed to balance growth.

Just as next time you find a £1 coin down the back of the sofa, you won't look with distrust at your furniture for stealing your hard earned cash, we shouldn't look with distrust at the welfare state or the NHS, or any other public service, for that matter. These are truly remarkable systems to be proud of. If – as science suggests – there is no afterlife, you have lived as a member of a species so advanced as to be capable of things that are utterly wonderful to behold. Things that you and other members of your species have fought tooth and nail for, died in pursuit of, and championed, whether popular or not. What better life could you have lived?

And it all starts with understanding why waste exists in any system, whilst not allowing yourself to see it out of context.

WHAT'S IN A WORD?

In season six of the excellent TV production satire, *30 Rock*, the protago-
nist – Liz Lemon – accidentally mobilises an organised group of protestors against her show. They become organised after she releases a
statement calling one of her star actors an 'idiot', for his previous homophobic comments. The group that mobilises against her? The self-
identifying 'idiot community'. As a result, she is warned to pacify the 'idiot
community' by her boss, as it makes up the largest bulk of her viewers.

Perhaps unintentionally, *30 Rock* references a growing problem in
some sections of ethical discussion. Following on from the rightful
demonising of racist, sexist and homophobic insults, many in the
community now champion the cause of anti-ableism. Ableist insults – like
referring to someone's lack of empathy as 'autistic', or someone who
makes unintelligible comments as a 'spaz' – can stigmatise and/or offend
people who hold the physical or mental characteristics that the insult is
meant to be capitalising on. It thus makes sense that we stigmatise use of
these words themselves, in the same way that we now stigmatise insults
like 'queer' or 'Paki'. It's all discrimination, and it's all potentially harmful.

Occasionally – and it is occasional – this 'political correctness' of campaigns against words goes off course. It does so in two main ways:
irrelevant extension of meaning, and irrelevant extension of grouping.

The first way – irrelevant extension of meaning – is where advocates
of equality mistakenly spot meaning in the use of a word where there is
none. For instance, whereas words like 'whore' or 'slut' are often used to
discriminate based on gender, advocates often extend this illegitimately
to include any insult/swear word which is also, in at least one definition,
related to women. These primarily involve names for female genitals,
such as the 'C' word (no, I'm not typing it; I'll get too many emails).
Advocates argue that using the c-word is sexist. Yet there is little reason
to suggest that this word is sexist in the same way as the words which
actually generalise and marginalise women, as the C word appears to be
removed from its meaning.

I would argue that the objectification and imagery in the term 'slut',
for example, is very definitely one related to and capitalising on the
generalisation about women's personalities. Whilst – in British culture, at

least – I think the c-word is simply used as a strong, angry swear word. I do not think that relation to female genitalia is either intended or pictured when using it. Neither do I think that is what causes the anger in the party using or being attacked with that piece of language. The C-word may well be used as another word for female genitalia, but I would argue that it has more than one meaning, just like calling someone a 'dick' does. Of course, this might be highly culturally relative.

The second way of losing course on political correctness is irrelevantly extending the groups to which offense is caused. This way is more in line with what *30 Rock* referenced. To find the term 'idiot' discriminatory is of course ridiculous, because nobody identifies or chooses to identify as an idiot in real life. Yet it isn't far from the kind of terminology which some advocates have begun opposing as inappropriate extensions of anti-ableism. Some of these advocates have attempted to stigmatise words such as 'psychotic', 'psychopathic', 'schizophrenic' and 'stupid'.

The first three of those, at least, are in one sense 'ableist'. But only in the sense that they do refer to mental disabilities – and by that, I mean deviations from the mental norm, as there is a sense in which we all suffer symptoms of psychopathy or schizophrenia, yet most of us wouldn't be diagnosed as psychopathic or schizophrenic.

However, whilst they fit that definition, most of their use doesn't qualify as 'ableist' because of its use in accurate terms. Calling someone 'schizo' would of course be unnecessary, ableist and offensive, as would the term 'psycho'. However, referring to a piece of uncompassionate action or behaviour as 'psychopathic' could be – and often is – entirely accurate. The same goes for behaviourally discontinuous acts being labelled schizophrenic. We all do exhibit occasional traits for these mental illnesses, and I'm unsure there is harm in pointing it out, unless we assume that those with mental health issues are in a completely different brain state to us. Which is itself offensive and untrue.

In fact, to pretend only diagnosed psychopaths or schizophrenic individuals suffer symptoms associated with these disorders, is to mischaracterise and isolate mental illness, ensuring that sufferers remain completely different from 'normal' people. We err by isolating these kinds of terms in an act of over-extension; we also harm the genuinely important cause of anti-discriminatory language.

Demonising the term 'stupid' is even more straight-cut. Yes, 'stupid' is a term used to reference a lack of intelligence, and, yes, some people do have a lack of intelligence. However, like with the illegitimate extensions in ableism, we all lack intelligence in some areas, and is it really wrong to reference this lack of intelligence? What's more – returning to *30 Rock*'s use of 'idiot' – does anyone actually self-identify as stupid? And if they do, is the fault in our use of the word making them feel offended? Or is it more to do with other instances in society making them feel stupid, worthless or unvalued? No one should feel 'stupid', because no one is 'stupid' in every way in which you could measure it.

This brings us to a final, important point. The problem with discriminatory language isn't, actually, that it offends. Offense is a necessary and vital thing to put up with in a free society. Offense is how new ideas are bought in, how old ideas are cast out, and how things like discrimination are first challenged. Indeed, without satire causing offence to the status quo, it is doubtful that change would ever occur. Satire is so often the form of media that popularises social change.

Discriminatory language is problematic because of the norms which it ingrains and passes on. Your elderly parents referring to the Asian couple who run the corner shop as 'Pakis' is – often unintentionally – a way of otherising them. Dismissing gay people as 'queers' is a way of creating a separate, alien group which you don't have to interact with. Using any ableist term to identify people you don't respect is an invisible way of degrading the status of the disabled. Insulting women based on their promiscuity – or lack of – is a way of ensuring their role below men, with whom there are no such derogatory terms. All of these are examples of what sociologists would call 'the ruling class' helping to pass normal beliefs (norms) from person to person, ensuring that things remain roughly as they are. Richard Dawkins would label these kinds of beliefs 'memes', which almost self-replicate, as the people holding the beliefs naturally help them to pass on to their groups as well. Only our explicit opposition and refusal to use these kinds of words is really effective at combating them.

What we do not need to oppose is every word that causes offence. If someone is showing a lack of intelligence about something – refusing to stop using sexist language, for instance, by using their own bias as an excuse – then I don't necessarily see the harm in labelling this behaviour stupid or idiotic, or even morally schizophrenic if they do see the value in refusing to use racist language but not sexist language. Of course, such a put down has no place in academic discussion – which is what advocates of social causes so often indulge in – and perhaps that is where they are confronted by confusion. Of course we shouldn't result to rude or offensive responses in academia, but academia isn't wider society. In wider society there is nothing wrong with satire or wit, and indeed the world would still be a fairly binary, illiberal place were it not for humans using this tactic to great effect previously.

WHY YOU SHOULDN'T DEMONISE ECONOMIC GROWTH

It's very appealing to criticise the idea of economic growth as being ethically vacant. The reason for that can be explained by a simple hypothetical. Imagine Earth consists of just ten very simple and reasonably financially similar nations. For one of these nations to enjoy growth – ie a larger proportional GDP (sum of national sales) – it is rationally attractive to believe that it must benefit at the expense of another nation.

This is, itself, easy to explain. We believe that growth consists of getting more of a share of an abstract pool of money/resources. So for one to do that, the line in the relevant pie chart must move so as to reduce someone else's share. This would appear to mean that economics is a zero sum game, meaning one person's benefit is always at the cost of another. Similarly, given that the majority of people increasing their wealth are already on the wealthy side, it would appear to logically entail that the zero sum game of economics is ethically bankrupt.

This is a half-truth. It certainly is true that those generally getting richer are those who are already quite rich. But this isn't a necessary problem of economic growth. If we go back to the example of the pie chart – where we thought about the believable idea that for your slice to grow, one of your fellows' slices must reduce – we can show a logical error, as that isn't the only way for your part of the pie to grow. The pie itself could grow, and your part of the corresponding growth in the global pie could be bigger than your fellows. This means that no one has dropped – no one has even stayed the same – but you have achieved growth without the expense of other nations.

How do you do this? Primarily, through inflation. If the value of a currency decreases, in a way that benefits you rather than others, you can be better off as a result. Without anyone else necessarily being worse off.

The more economic-minded among you will be thinking suspiciously at this stage. Sure, inflation can essentially create value out of nothing – financially speaking – but that still has a real world effect. If one currency decreases in value, out of kilter with other currencies in a way which causes significant inflation, then someone is holding resources/finances of less worth as a result. In other words, if your currency is worth more, someone else's currency is worth less.

This is absolutely right. But there's no reason that this has to be immoral. Clever government policies can use growth, and methods such as inflation, as a system of mild wealth redistribution. You don't need a revolution, or even any massive evolution, to make society fairer: if you decrease the value of the currency that people already own, you create an opportunity for those with less to catch up. As the value of currency drops, as a global relative, new businesses and workers in that country have a chance to catch up with those that already have wealth in the old money.

Of course, growth isn't necessarily a tool for wealth distribution any more than it's necessarily a tool for increasing inequality. At the moment it is certainly used much more for the latter. This is as we allow for banking and other financial systems to favour those with wealth; those using growth to become wealthier at the expense of the non-wealthy. But if used correctly, economic growth can be a great tool for gradually and fairly addressing that balance. The ethical economic problem is not growth itself.

About the Author

Robert A Johnson is a practical ethicist and philosopher of science, who graduated in Mental Philosophy from the University of Aberdeen. He specialises in the intersection of morality and rationality, whilst being a staunch advocate of science and evidence-based endeavours. His other interests and work lie primarily in animal ethics, where he has written numerous articles on animal welfare and animal rights, whilst standing up for non-human interests from a rational perspective.

For more information visit www.robertjohnson.org.uk or find him on Facebook @RationalMorality

About the Illustrator

Chuck Harrison is an illustrator and writer who lives with his son called Puff and his cat named Monkey in New York. His caffeine fuelled works have been printed by DC Comics, Color Ink Book, The South Wedge Quarterly and in many other fine publications.

For more information visit iLikeChuckHA.com

www.ingramcontent.com/pod-product-compliance
Lightning Source LLC
Chambersburg PA
CBHW060014050426
42448CD00012B/2744